SWITCH

Wishing you health, happiness and great conversation in 2021.

Paul.

SWITCH

from telling to trusting with
powerful leader conversations

Paul Matthews

Published by Paul Matthews

First published in 2020 in Sydney, Australia

Copyright © Paul Matthews

www.paulmatthews.com.au
16 Commodore St
Newtown 2042, Australia

Edited by Jenny Magee

Typeset, printed and bound in Australia by BookPOD

ISBN: 978-0-6488689-0-3 (pbk)
ISBN: 978-0-6488689-1-0 (ebook)

A catalogue record for this
book is available from the
National Library of Australia

NATIONAL
LIBRARY
OF AUSTRALIA

For Mum and Dad.
Thank you.

Acknowledgments

Over the years, I have learnt a great deal from many leaders from all over the world. Much of their wisdom is included in this book. Special thanks to those I have interviewed recently, including Michael Schneider, Angela Tsoutakos, John Banfield, Simon Harris, Ted Stuckey, Alex Goryachev and Bronwyn Evans.

Many friends have supported, nudged and sometimes shoved me along on this trip. Thanks to Mary Butler for lighting the way, to Callum McKirdy, Emma McQueen and Alex Hagan for their belief and support. Thanks to many others in my tribe for being so sure that I would, when I was not even sure that I could.

I am a better person, and my world is a brighter place because of my beautiful wife, Rhian. She has been there every single step of my adult life, throughout my career and at my side whilst I wrote this book. Thank you for believing in me and for your love and support.

Contents

Introduction

'What if you end up half-dead in a ditch?' my Mum had asked. And ten days later that's exactly where I was – bleeding out, half-dead in deepest, darkest Karnataka, Southern India.

Our bus to Goa ran into one of India's sacred cows, and we rolled off the road at high speed in the dark, landing upside-down in the jungle. We were lucky to be alive. Some didn't make it.

I had a deep head wound and was bleeding profusely.

Instantly my wife and I put our wellbeing in the hands of the locals. With no option but to trust them, my survival was utterly reliant on their knowledge, skills and kindness.

Depending on our own ideas and experiences would have meant disaster. We had to adapt quickly to the local conditions and needs of our situation. Dialling 000 was not an option or even possible.

By trusting others, we enlisted their support, action, energy and instincts, and that got us to safety.

Evolved leaders trust

Thankfully, we rarely find ourselves bleeding out or lost in the jungle. But we do face daily challenges that require us to trust others to thrive and survive in business. Yet too often in these situations, leaders often resort to telling others what needs to be done, instead of trusting. They focus on their own solutions, because deep down, and for whatever reason, they believe they know best.

Building team trust and enlisting their support requires leaders to evolve their communication strategies. To let go of the old ways of telling, and instead, give power to others, so they can bring their knowledge and skills to resolve daily challenges.

I see evolved leaders building trust and creating rich outcomes on the back of it. They have learnt the value of empowering others, rather than telling them what to do.

Work, the workforce and the workplace have changed. In the 2020s, employees both expect and need trusting communication from leaders. But many leaders have not yet caught up and consequently are holding themselves and their teams back, depriving their business of the very ideas and solutions that could propel it forward.

Trusting more and telling less is a switch from which every leader can benefit. So, here is my challenge to you. As you walk through these pages, consider how you can move away from the old ways of telling, that instil control and limits. How can you trust others more and use their insights and ideas to advance?

If you can't communicate you can't lead

The way we communicate affects our outcomes. It's like a roof – trust raises the roof and your results; telling lowers and restricts them. I firmly believe that if your communication doesn't empower your team, then you cannot lead effectively.

But I hear you say...

- No one taught me how to communicate
- I haven't been trained to build trust
- Telling works fine in my team
- My team are used to being told
- Telling is quicker and more efficient.

These are direct quotes from leaders in organisations I work with — and at face value, they might seem true. But they also reflect the frustrations expressed in annual cycles of employee engagement surveys, where employees ask for:

- More involvement
- Better communication
- More leader visibility
- More collaboration
- More innovation.

I've no doubt these reasons (and excuses) have real impacts on business. They occur across all industries, at all levels and in public and private sectors. But given they keep coming up, year after year, with little change, I feel it's time to break the cycle. Trusting is our way of doing things differently to get a different and much better result.

When solved (or even improved), we see dramatic and positive impacts on the entire business. Yet many of these problems remain unsolved. They keep coming back – often justified through lack of budget, change resistance or the complex nature of business. Many organisations have firmly held beliefs that 'communication is always a big problem' or 'employees always say leaders lack visibility' or (my favourite) 'there will always be a lack of trust in management'.

That doesn't have to be the case. Solving these issues is possible. Improvement is not simple, but it is straightforward and can happen on a significant scale. I have seen the evidence when trust increases, and leaders proactively involve others.

Just imagine

What could *you* as a leader achieve with greater trust, more ideas and support from a workforce that went above and beyond because they felt valued and involved? What would the impact and results mean for you as a leader?

A 2017 Gallup workplace poll reported that only 15 per cent of employees in the Western workforce is engaged (Gallup, 2017). My goal is to help leaders change this. Raising this figure by even one per cent could save hundreds of billions of dollars. Imagine what could be achieved globally if employees were safer, more innovative, efficient and customer-focused. What it takes is trust.

This book shows how leaders – just like you – can significantly improve outcomes through trusting conversations. The examples you'll read are from my interviews with many leaders across retail, utilities, government, finance, transport, logistics, advertising and beyond. Trusting conversations raise leader results across every sector and industry. Every time.

Is Switch for you?

Don't read any further if you want to continue to tell your employees what to do. If you enjoy sending them those vanilla corporate messages and generally accept your current results, then Switch is not for you.

Move on if you are one of those bosses who is happy to measure employee engagement but wants to tick a box that makes it all go away. That's what I consider the old way of leading. This book is for leaders who are serious about upping the ante and getting better results.

Do read on if you want to understand your employees, unite and excite your team, support them, do a great job and achieve outstanding results. And feel good about it along the way.

If you want to get under the skin of your workforce, improve your leadership, increase performance and see real change, then buckle up and get ready to change.

Good, I'm glad we have got that clear, right from the start. Clarity is so important.

How this book works

Switch is structured in two parts, with nine chapters.

In **Part One**, we'll explore the challenges leaders face when communicating with employees, recognising that the most successful leaders have moved from telling employees what to do, towards a more trusting style of communication. We'll examine the need for leaders to consistently evolve to meet the needs of their teams in a more complex world of work. Then we'll explore the importance of communication in leading and see how it can limit or lift results, team performance and outcomes across the whole business. We'll run the numbers on the cost of communication and note the dramatic and long-lasting impacts of getting better at conversations.

Part Two is a practical walkthrough of the powerful conversations approach. Each step guides with practical insights, stories and examples that will shift your focus so you can build trust and achieve greater impact and results.

Each chapter explains how to create a step-change towards powerful conversations. Following a 3-2-1 format inspired by James Clear (a global authority on building good habits), each chapter concludes with five takeaway points, three questions and an inspirational quote, to help you Switch. This provides a quick summary of actions that build trust and reduce telling.

One more thing, before we start. It's useful for us to share an understanding of the key terms you'll encounter in the book.

Communication is the process of sharing information to increase understanding between people or groups of people. It's pretty important for leaders. We'll focus on two forms of communication:

Telling is one-way communication, where one person sends information to another, from A to B in a single direction.

Conversation is two-way communication involving the exchange of information between two or more people. It goes back and forth and is based on listening, responding and understanding.

Conversation builds understanding. This leads to **connection** between humans. When we communicate through conversation, we understand each other better, and our relationship deepens far more than when we tell each other what to do.

The greater the connection a leader has with their team, the greater their impact or results.

Now, let's explore why these things matter so much and get ready to Switch.

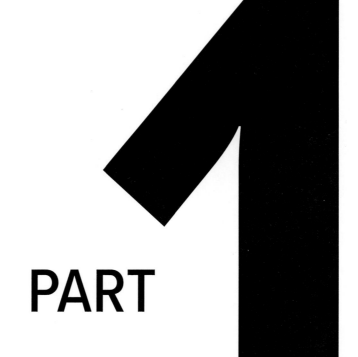

PART

Why Switch?

Welcome!

The first part of the book explains the importance of communication to leaders and organisations and why recent changes mean we need to lead differently. This switch is driven by new thinking and evidence, and by the evolution of the workforce and its changed business structures.

I'll highlight a compelling case for why organisations and their managers should shift to a more inclusive way of leading and communicating. These chapters show how moving away from our old ways of hierarchy and telling, towards conversations is a highly effective way to build greater impact and bigger results.

Chapter One explores the evolution of our workforce, the three critical challenges this brings for leaders and how neuroscience can guide your communication style.

Chapter Two outlines how leaders influence business performance, behaviour and culture, making their communication a big deal when it comes to influencing employees and business outcomes.

Chapter Three is all about the data of communication. We examine the cost of poor communication on businesses (including yours!), and show how to lift productivity and profit with the simplest of changes.

Chapter Four explores four different types of leader communication styles. In this chapter, we climb the ladder of impact to see how communication capability and style can lift results, growing trust and engagement, or reduce effort and impact in our teams.

1

The Challenges of Communicating in the 2020s

Imagine you have bright ideas, thoughts and energy that could help others and make things better. How would it feel to be ignored, excluded or trusted?

Throughout the 20th century, the business community built grand hierarchies, paid the occupants plenty of money and called them managers. The best and brightest sat at the top of the corporate pyramid. Revered and influential because of their technical expertise or length of service, they controlled employees by telling them how to do things. This 'Age of Telling' was a time when challenging a leader, suggesting alternative actions or having ideas of your own was unlikely to be a positive employee experience.

Thankfully this culture of delegation and superiority is fading, but it is not yet over. The essence still survives in many cultures and leaders style of communication.

That's why I have written this book — to help businesses and leaders evolve in line with the needs of the current workforce. I want them to use the latest evidence to get the very best from their employees. Switch is a move from *telling* employees what to do, to *trusting* them to use their strengths, insights, experience and ideas to achieve a better outcome.

Work has been de-humanised

We are all humans with imagination and ideas. Yet for some reason, we've spent more than a century de-humanising our working lives. The very activity that consumes most of our waking time is divested of the qualities and comforts that humans value. Entire working lives and careers have passed without recognition of unique traits that are now regarded as essential to progress and advancement.

We de-humanised workplaces so much that, from the 1950s, we painted a vision where robots replaced people. How wrong we were. That imagined scenario was de-personalised, emotion-free and hierarchical: not fun or enjoyable and exclusive. It favoured leaders and their ideas but burdened them with obligation and expectations of results.

Personality, character and imagination are all recognised as beneficial for work in the 2020s and beyond (Pistrui, 2018). That's in stark contrast to the robots we dreamed up in the 1950s. But we spent years telling employees to leave their feelings and emotions at the door, keep their personal lives separate, hide feelings and ideas, and do as they were told. Even now, many industries or businesses still value hierarchy, impersonality and bureaucracy over employee ideas and innovations. They are falling behind because they fail to listen, take on new ways or adapt to the needs of the workforce. The Gallup figure mentioned earlier, of just 15 per cent of employees engaged at work, should come as no surprise.

Would you engage with a leader who fails to listen, trust or ask?

We know now that hierarchy, depersonalisation and telling hold business back. Emotional intelligence (EQ), character, feelings and mental health are closely linked to productivity and results (Entrepreneur, 2017). Like it or not, our home and work lives are entwined. It's no longer a question of leaving home or personality at the office door, as we are increasingly empowered to be ourselves at work: parent, sibling, grandparent – even dog owner. We go to work as individuals with ideas and experiences that create value. With many employees now working from home, this is a far cry from times past.

Examples, anecdotes and evidence prove that feelings and emotions are a vital part of high performance and better productivity at work. We value emotional intelligence and see that those leaders who have it, get better results (Dollard, 2018). EQ is widely regarded as the best way to lead (Morse, 2018).

Moving on from the age of telling, we are torn between telling our employees what to do and trusting them to do the right thing. We want to empower them and build engagement, but we can't always let go. We want to build trust, but also to get things right the first time and not be seen as too 'hands-off' or making mistakes. We want to recognise our employees as human, but ultimately we believe they are there to work hard and get strong results – no matter what.

Evolving our leadership to meet the needs of the workforce has never been as crucial as it is now.

The 2020s: It's time to trust

Here's the thing. It's the 2020s, and we are in the process of re-humanising our leadership and business. Our workforce has evolved and is highly educated. Workplaces are changing and often at a distance. Work itself has transformed, and hierarchy has become counter-productive in many companies. Globally, leaders are finding they have no option but to let go of the past and involve their team far more than before. The remote workforce means trusting others to do a good job, not trying to control or solve all of the issues ourselves.

It's timely, then, that leaders evolve and move away from a place of control and telling. The workforce wants to be trusted, involved, listened to and held accountable. Employees want to be seen as humans, not just workers. Alongside their employers, they expect leaders to nurture personality, imagination and contribution. If leaders cannot have meaningful, connected and productive conversations with their colleagues, then they are limiting productivity and results.

This new generation of leaders is now expected to set a direction and channel energy towards achieving goals. They no longer need to have high technical expertise or be able to command and control an army. Technical credibility has been replaced with the need to excite and unite the workforce. This requires a trusting approach, not a telling one. This switch is driven by an educated workforce that wants to have a voice and be involved. They want to be part of the solution. They don't expect their leaders to have all the answers or solve all the problems, as that is part of the attraction of work.

The challenges for today's leaders

This book sets out a proven way to build communication as the *how* of leadership in our era, that will nurture trust and involve employees. The results of this switch can be breathtaking, as we will learn in the coming pages. But before we get into the results, let's explore some of the challenges we face as leaders in the 2020s.

Challenge One: Evolving

Recent changes in the way we work and the composition of our workforce are essential factors in improving how we communicate and lead. To build connection and trust, we must tailor our communication to needs that have changed significantly over recent years. Work, the workforce and the workplace have come a long way.

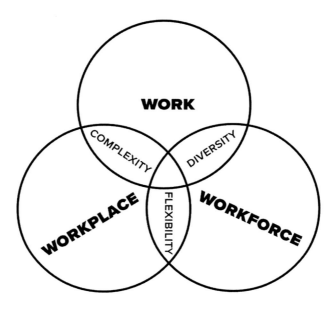

Figure 1: Evolution at work

More complexity

We are experiencing change at a faster pace than ever before – this is certainly so in the businesses I have worked in over the last decade. Keeping up with these changes is a real challenge. Many organisations and leaders are facing change fatigue caused by constant transformation. Some say that leaders need to evolve to survive, and I agree that there is no going back. There is unlikely to be a slowing down of change. It is the new normal.

Over recent years work has changed in many ways:

- New roles and teams
- New policies and protocols to implement or manage such as social media or big data

- New ways of working, e.g. agile environments
- New products and services, e.g. apps and data management
- New technology and devices, e.g. artificial intelligence or automation
- New regulation, e.g. e-laws, worker and environmental protection
- New practices, e.g. remote or home working
- New ways to lead and manage emergencies, e.g. bushfires or pandemics.

Leading is a very different beast to what it was a decade ago, with further change never far away. The use of technology, big data and significant disruption to industries and sectors has changed how we work. Forever. These demographic changes have driven change on so many fronts. Working from home, remote working, agile working and other practices are now firmly established as the norm – especially since the 2020 pandemic. All of this creates a challenging environment for effective communication between leaders and teams. If our leadership doesn't adapt and evolve, then communication, impact and results will suffer.

More diverse workforce

More people are working than ever before. Research by McCrindle helps us understand how the demography of our employees has changed and what this means for us as leaders. Workforces now often include up to five generations, each with their particular preferences and needs (McCrindle, n.d.).

The older ones (born before 1964)

Research shows that older generations of employees differ markedly from their younger peers. While this might sound obvious, these differences are important for leading.

Older workers (Baby Boomers and Builders) have grown up with a controlling style of leadership. They are more likely to respond to leaders who think and command. They respond to structure and formal environments when learning and prefer expert opinions. They rely on authority for information. That said, their preferences are adapting as younger people enter leadership roles and are less inclined to work or lead in the same way as older colleagues. These preferences at work are also reducing as these generations leave the workforce over time.

Generation X (born 1965-1979)

Those who are currently, or nearing, middle-aged, prefer a coordinating leadership style, that is less commanding. Their preference is for a leader who does, not tells, and they would rather learn through participation. Taking part and being involved is a key engager for this group and a way for them to develop.

Gen X seek involvement to create belonging at work. They take influence from practitioners – those who are involved and get stuff done. They are inspired by leaders who are closely connected to their team, understand the work and can advise or coordinate.

They are a large cohort of the current workforce and make up a significant part of the leadership teams of businesses operating right now. Gen X is the leadership team of the future and vital to ensuring that younger generations are more involved.

Generation Y and Z (born since 1980)

By 2030, 67 per cent of the Australian workforce will have been born after 1980. Significantly better educated than previous generations, they are more open in their views and share them easily. This large part of the workforce is digitally savvy and empowered (McCrindle, n.d.).

Younger workers respond better to inclusion and involvement by leaders. They look to their peers for influence and are informed by online and group forums, and social media. Information is sought on their terms from trusted sources, rather than from authority (e.g. celebrities rather than expert or political leaders). Trust is an essential currency for successful leadership of this group.

In writing this book, I've had conversations with leaders and CEOs across the world who have been generous with their thoughts. Look for their observations and experiences throughout these pages.

❝ I feel as though the younger demographic are not willing just to take information and go and beaver away anymore. They want to be part of the conversation. Younger people now are also much more ambitious and want to move up the organisation quickly – which I quite like now that I am used to it. There is an expectation that their aspirations are taken seriously by leaders. ❞

– Bronwyn Evans, CEO, Engineers Australia

Much has been written about the work-based needs of Gen Y (Millennials). As with every generation, they have specific needs. But what sets them apart is the degree to which they are empowered.

Gen Y started work in a much more educated and prosperous era. They are more technologically sophisticated than any previous cohort of employees. Digitally literate, they are used to contributing their views with ease, online and in person. Having evolved in a more open learning environment, they are more at ease with challenging the status quo at work or suggesting alternative ways of doing things. They are conditioned to challenge, having grown up in an age of change and disruption.

Gen Y are helping drive another industrial revolution and, in turn, are changing the way businesses are run. I find this fascinating, but it can be confronting for leaders who don't understand the needs of Gen Y and are unable to communicate or engage with them.

Gen Z (born between 1995 and 2009) make up a small portion of the current workforce, but their preferences already show a continued trend for more involvement and conversation by leaders. Their leadership style is empowering – the opposite of telling and control. Their ideal leader is a collaborator, and their preferred learning style is multi-modal. All this tells us that greater immersion of employees in conversation and dialogue is a vital skill now and moving forward for leaders.

The dynamic workplace

As work and the workforce evolve, so does our workplace. The rigid policies and systems that underpinned organisations of the past were fit for then, but not the 2020s. We work very differently now, so we need to lead and communicate differently, too.

The 2020 workplace has evolved beyond recognition in comparison to times where telling was the way to lead. Employees then sought a job for life, working set or consistent hours in an agreed location. Employment conditions were typically stricter with more rigid expectations of employers. Structure and consistency were an effective way of creating more reliability and high performance from employees. The expectations of employees and employers are different now.

Our definition of a productive workplace has changed. The organisation of workspaces has moved away from formal systems that require us to attend the office daily, clock in or sit at an allocated desk. Instead, appreciation of the need for collaboration and social interaction at work has led to systems of hot-desking, open plan and now more agile environments. Our workplace design underpins the importance of communication and involvement at work.

Changes in technology mean many industries can work from multiple locations, away from their operations or assets. Working from home is now commonplace in most corporate organisations. The 2020 pandemic has forced businesses to rely on working at home to stay safe from infection. Further changes to the workplace are imminent because of this.

Many employers now realise that they no longer need to pay high rents and costs to house their workforce in expensive offices, when working at home is accepted as the new way of work.

How we lead and communicate needs to evolve in line with our dynamic workplaces. Employees are more remote, rely more on technology and require less supervision than before. Leaders who recognise this are more likely to evolve and get better results.

Leadership hierarchies are changing

Traditional hierarchies and delegation of tasks are rapidly replaced with blurred lines. By this, I mean that the linear cascade of communication from leaders limits their outcomes because it doesn't take the audience into account. Instead, internal networks and social interaction across teams and informal communication are replacing the long-established rigid cascade system. Leaders need to be more connected, open, transparent and consultative.

Workplace communication has evolved too. Previous hierarchies focused on authority, superiority and control of information as the way to lead and communicate, and this now applies far less.

Inspiring and coaching employees has become a more effective way to ensure relevance as a leader and to deliver results in a complex workforce. That is why *conversations* have become more crucial to results than telling. Leadership that gets the best out of the 2020 workforce is more concerned with inspiring and enabling, and that requires conversations.

Leaders who don't evolve

Leaders who have not moved with these changes will likely continue to focus on hierarchy and control. But that is limiting their results. In the next chapter, we'll explain why this is so, but before you move on, consider research done by Gallup, explained in the following table. It helps us understand what motivates today's workforce (Gandhi, 2018).

Historically employees were more motivated by their pay, their boss and working on their weaknesses. These days, most of our workforce values purpose, conversations and a life outside of work as motivators for success. This is significant food for thought for leaders who continue to operate as they did a decade or so ago.

Factors that motivate employees	
The Past	The Future
My Paycheck	My Purpose
My Satisfaction	My Development
My Boss	My Coach
My Annual Review	My Ongoing Conversations
My Weaknesses	My Strengths
My Job	My Life

Table 1: Factors that motivate employees

Are we more connected or more distracted?

Constant change has brought new ways for employees and leaders to become more connected. It can also create barriers for leaders as our audience becomes distracted. While our love affair with the mobile phone, apps and social media has created significant opportunities and growth, it has created another obstacle for leaders, employers and brands to have to 'cut through' to harness the energy of their teams effectively.

We face a feast of information and a famine of attention – at the same time.

This level of change and connection happens both in and outside work, presenting a compelling case for leaders to communicate through trust, not telling. Keeping teams focused on the day-to-day work, let alone key business priorities, is more challenging than ever.

Stock-take

Consider the changes you have experienced at work over the last decade and list them below:

New technologies

_____

_____

_____

_____

New ways of working

_____

_____

_____

_____

_____

New roles or teams

_____

_____

_____

_____

_____

How have you changed your leadership and communication to accommodate these?

_____

_____

_____

_____

_____

Challenge Two: Involving

The question of whether or not to involve employees is all but obsolete. Involvement is now a fundamental expectation of most of the workforce. The way leaders go about doing so limit or lift their success and results.

Hardwired to engage

Most employees, especially younger ones, are hardwired to have their say and want to get involved. Education at school, college and university ensured they had an immersive experience, contributing views and ideas as a way of learning through conversation, not traditional lectures. These days failure and discourse are increasingly valued as ways to grow towards success. Taking part is the norm for new entrants to the world of work. They have rarely been told what to do and expect to be respected and trusted.

Learning systems since the 1990s include involvement and experimentation as a way to involve learners in conversations and experiences. Gap years, role plays, design and build projects, and other hands-on learnings have helped shape a generation of employees that want in. More recently, access to tech, data and global learning systems has removed the need for individuals to be highly qualified or privileged to have a voice or be heard.

Most homes in the West have internet access, and most employees have smartphones, ensuring they can voice their views in real-time, all day long, on any issue they are passionate about (including their employers or leaders!). For them, freely sharing their views and opinions at work is no different from doing so at home.

All these factors have cemented an expectation in the minds of employees that employers and leaders will also involve them at work. Going to school for 15 years, then to university, equips employees with a hardwired lust to change things and challenge ways. They want to have and use their views and ideas to help solve work problems. After all, isn't that why they were hired?

I find it baffling that almost every set of employee engagement survey results still shows people screaming out for more involvement. Most surveys show that employees think the business needs to improve one or more of the following:

- Leadership and leader visibility
- Communication
- Transparency or decision-making
- Collaboration or teamwork
- Innovation.

These themes come up continually over successive years at some businesses. My concern is that leaders need to be far more open and involve their employees. By 2028 most new employees in the market will have a university degree. Greater employee involvement would significantly address all of the issues listed above.

Stock-take

- Does your employee data or feedback reflect these issues?
- What behaviours or conditions do you think are driving these results?
- Are you personally solving or adding to these problems?

The involvement problem

Employees and leaders get excited by doing good work, making a difference and resolving issues. Curious by nature, it helps us to focus. But problems are only inspiring when employees feel empowered to help solve them – and that requires them to be involved and invited in by leaders.

However, many leaders I work with still feel the need to solve all the problems themselves. They find themselves fighting fires or sorting out issues. Because they are always solving problems, they can't let go. That's ironic given feedback that employees don't feel involved in decision-making, that innovation or ideas are few and far between, or that communication is poor.

Switching to a more inclusive leadership style will create greater involvement by leaders. It will free up leader time, creating more space for them to work *on* the business, instead of *in* it. Letting go absolves leaders of having to fix every problem in their teams.

Communication as the 'how' of leadership

Many leaders believe that solving the communication conundrum mentioned above or creating more employee involvement requires much time and extra work. They worry it will channel their efforts away from their real work. The opposite is true.

These same leaders tell me they don't trust their employees to do the job as well as they could. They feel they have to be involved for things to stay on track and that if they let go, things won't get resolved. They lack trust.

The reality is that changing how leaders communicate and involve, resolves a lot of other business challenges – improvements in communication yield significant results in collaboration and innovation. It accelerates other outcomes such as change, innovation and customer scores. The price of better communication capability for leaders is tiny in comparison with the cost of the waste and inertia caused by low involvement or micromanagement.

Communication is not an optional extra

Leaders who have embedded communication deliver more positive results because employees get involved – they see communication as part of leading. They include employees and have conversations as part of the daily routine. It's not left out or forgotten as an optional extra. Recognising and focusing on communication as part of the job elevates results.

When communication is part of how they lead, they can engage with their teams with ease, driving positive results. That consistent level of contact builds meaningful relationships that lock in trust.

Leadership that involves employees has proved to be a significant contributor to successful transformation and change globally. Conversations that generate involvement are priceless for businesses. They activate ideas, improvement, opinions and energy that transform and create in a way and on a scale that leaders on their own simply cannot.

> ❝ If leaders can't communicate then they can't build a movement. Getting support behind an idea or problem is so incredibly important. Communication has to be front and centre. So many ideas and solutions never make it because leaders or organisations were unable to communicate them effectively. It's a vital skill. ❞
> — *Ted Stuckey, MD, QBE Ventures*

Empower employees: they know their stuff best

In an interview with John Banfield, CEO of BPAY, I asked how they involve and empower their employees. He said they work hard to cultivate a collaborative, inclusive culture where everyone is inspired and empowered to be their best. Innovation, collaboration and customer-centricity is part of their DNA.

'I had a recent example of a software change. Ahead of that happening on a weekend, we were trying to decide if we should go ahead with the change. The leader brought the decision to me and the leadership team for the final OK to proceed. I asked lots of questions: How long has it been planned? Have we informed customers? How confident are we that this is going to work? I told the CIO that this decision is yours and the team's, not mine. You are the best person to make this decision. I trust you. The team were empowered and autonomous. They put their best foot forward, and it succeeded.

We previously had an 'Ad-hoc-racy culture' where some of the elements were great. There was a clan culture too, where some leaders on the team were seen as parents. We have now moved to a place where leaders are seen as coaches or mentors, which is much more productive and empowering for employees.

We eventually moved our engagement scores from 59 per cent to 93 per cent engagement in about four years. A big part of that has come from employees being empowered, accountable and aligned.'

Control reduces your impact and effectiveness

Author and science journalist Daniel Goleman wrote that a leader's power and impact decreases with every initiative they seek to control. Controlling leaders negatively impact company climate. Flexibility and innovation get hit really hard by needless control by leaders. Extreme top-down decision-making kills new ideas on the vine. People feel so disrespected that they think, 'I won't even bring my ideas up – they'll only be shot down.'

As Goleman said, people's sense of responsibility evaporates. Unable to act on their own initiative, they lose their sense of ownership and feel little accountability for their performance. Some become so resentful they adopt the attitude, 'I'm not going to help this bastard' (Goleman, 2000).

The question of whether or not to involve employees is all but obsolete. Involvement is a fundamental expectation – *how* leaders and organisations do so sets the ceiling for success.

The ceiling of what is possible for a leader rises as they empower others to contribute. The more inclusive and open you are as a company or as a leader, the greater your potential for impact and results. This is what has led me to believe so strongly that communication and employee engagement leads to limitless potential – as long as leaders create the right conditions (Sostrin, 2017).

Challenge Three: Connecting

Telling employees what to do creates a profoundly different response in their brain than involving them in conversation or problem-solving. The outcomes are different too.

Let's explore what goes on in the brain and then consider how this plays out at work.

In an article in *Psychology Today*, Balboa and Glaser wrote, 'By understanding how the brain functions, communicates and responds to our environment, we can reach our full potential... Conversations are not just a way of sharing information; they trigger physical and emotional changes in the brain that either open you up to having healthy, trusting conversations or close you down so you speak from fear, caution and anxiety' (Balboa, 2019).

Fight or flight – or bonding and alignment?

Neuroscience (the study of the brain) shows that telling employees provokes a stress-like response. They experience a flight or fight response that is similar to threats or fear.

In this *telling* situation, the employee's brain reacts, and the instinct is to shut down. Consequently, when leaders tell, employees retreat and enter compliance mode. They simply do as they are told as they don't feel empowered to bring their ideas and solutions to the situation. This is a sorry situation for the many employees who are highly experienced or educated and longing for involvement. They get deflated and won't trust us.

Telling limits team solutions because it requires the leader to be right. They drive compliance with their ideas, excluding the notion that others might know more or have different or better suggestions. It's an old-fashioned way to lead that reduces employee effort and success, limiting opportunity and thinking. When leaders tell, they lessen others' ability to trust them – the ultimate losing scenario for a leader, employee and business.

Trust gets amplified during employee conversations because they feel included — as though they matter and have value to add.

Contrast the situation above with the brain response experienced during a two-way conversation that involves and builds trust.

When we start a conversation with employees, their brain opens up and creates a desire to help. They are far more likely to trust leaders who involve them and ask questions. The brain reacts by creating a bonding response that connects with the person they are working with. The natural reaction for employees in this scenario is to contribute, take ownership and solve issues.

When the bonding reaction occurs during a conversation, employees bring more to work and add much more value. Conversations create an empowered feeling in the employee and lead to engagement and high-performance behaviour.

Conversations also yield insights in the form of different perspectives. They ignite options, enabling us to explore different views. Leaders who open up conversations and explore options create opportunities, drive ideas and enhance the status quo. They generate diversity of thought by listening to others. The outcome is the development of trust between leader and employee, magnifying the opportunity for success. That is why trust is so important; without it, we make our jobs and those of others more difficult.

Domination and delegation

Dominant behaviours, such as telling or giving orders, create stress. These inhibit the brain and reduce our desire to work with others. Our discretionary effort reduces – impacting results at work. It can affect wellbeing, which is accepted as a significant factor in productivity.

We are social animals. From an evolutionary perspective, attachment to others matters. Research suggests that a sense of connection can also impact productivity and emotional well-being. Scientists have found that emotions are contagious in the workplace. Employees can feel emotionally depleted just by watching unpleasant interactions between co-workers. If they see others being told what to do or shouted at, they think this is what is expected or will happen to them too.

Creating a connection through conversation is one of a leader's most important jobs. Once employees feel safe to be involved, they feel cared for and able to think and act more freely. This condition unleashes greater trust and potential in the team (Giles, 2016).

The age of telling is over

The leadership paradigm of telling might once have seemed an efficient way to run the armed forces – and in certain emergencies, it can still be valid. However, the telling approach is rapidly being replaced with a more open and inspirational leadership method based on conversations and involvement. Leaders globally are switching their communication style and seeing better results.

Command and control were considered effective when information and education were scarce, employee mobility non-existent, and business culture was based more on hierarchy than collaboration and transparency.

Delegation (telling) worked when leaders were viewed as superior to employees or deemed to know better. But in the new context, they aren't, and they don't. That's why the commanding leadership approach is now widely regarded as a negative and destructive way to run a business. More than ever, the delegation of tasks to junior team members is becoming a thing of the past. Instead, we value collective discussion, effort and focus as yielding better results.

Command and control worked well in 'the age of telling'. That was when leaders permitted others lower in the hierarchy to perform tasks the leader deemed suitable for their grade. They relied on the traditional cascade of information down the business – this linear, controlling approach limited impact and outcomes. Hierarchical communication in this way will die out in the 2020s. It is the white rhino of leadership, and it's easy to understand why the coercive style is the least effective in most situations (Goleman, 2000).

Lifting the ceiling of leader impact

Command and control approaches were based on the premise that leaders could solve all the problems in the business. It's unrealistic – if only because we are so caught up in the level of change and transformation. I often remind my clients that their employees know the business and customers best, so let them solve the problems.

No leader can do everything. Therefore, it's critical to distribute power throughout the organisation and to rely on decision-making from those who are closest to the action: i.e., the front-line employees. Our style of communication or leadership is like a ceiling and can limit how effective we are. Research has repeatedly shown that two-way communication creates empowered teams. These are more productive and proactive, provide better customer service, and offer higher levels of job satisfaction and commitment to their organisation (Giles, 2016).

Macho over-achievement

When I started work in the 1990s corporate world, I was told that failure was not an option. Leaders used this line to scare us into working harder and doing our best no matter what. Now we know that fear is not the best way to motivate.

Over the last twenty years, my experience has shown that failure is integral to learning and that it's OK to fail as long as we try our best. It's a very different sentiment to when control and perfection were the endgames. I now know, and evidence clarifies, that instilling fear in employees is not motivating, big or clever. It doesn't work. Those 1980s and 90s macho symbols of corporate over-achievement are no longer relevant in creating high performance in our teams. They are increasingly falling away from how leaders produce results.

Instead of fear and control, the current workforce and businesses value a more iterative approach, where we improve as we go, and take different views and people with us.

When it comes to communicating and engaging a team, employees want leaders to listen and take their views on board. That's the way to connect and get the best out of your team in the 2020s. This is a significant aspect of trusting leader conversations that we will explore throughout this book.

REFLECT

Work, the workforce and the workplace have evolved

Five Takeaways:

- Our workforce has evolved, so must we
- Work has evolved too: more change, more tech, more complexity
- Employees want to be involved and have their say
- Telling and orders shut employees down, limit results and outcomes
- Conversations build trust and get better results

Three Questions:

- What do I need to change to better align with the needs of my team?
- How can I create more conversations with my team and workforce?
- How can I involve employees more and lift my results?

One Quote:

❝ The most effective managers realize that they work for their teams and not the other way around. ❞
– *Google Research (Google, n.d.).*

2

Why Leader Communication is SO Important

Here we'll explore the significant contribution leaders make to business culture, performance and employee behaviour. In this chapter, we'll also gauge our style of leadership communication to see if we are telling, teasing, tentative or trusting with our employees.

Leaders build the culture of a business. Indeed, every employee impacts the culture and results, but leaders are the most influential party. And that influence plays out in your communication style.

If you are open to ideas, ask questions and seek input to help make improvements, then so too will your team. But if you are closed, if you shut people down or don't concern yourself with making things better, then most likely your team won't either.

There's nothing new in this finding. Various versions of an old proverb say a fish rots from the head. It suggests that if the leader is negative, then those following them will be too. And if a business fails, then it's likely caused by its leadership.

Culture makers

For better or for worse, leaders are undoubtedly the primary source of influence at work. Technology, tools and environment have an impact on employee experience and behaviour, but leaders are the dominant influence. Their communication impacts levels of performance, engagement and culture. Their involvement in decision-making and direction-setting makes them the big decider when it comes to workforce productivity and behaviour. We all know the saying about employees leaving bad bosses, not companies, right?

Leaders who connect with employees and involve them, positively influence organisational culture and dramatically influence business outcomes, change and reputation.

Be the person you want others to be

Workforce satisfaction and performance is undoubtedly influenced by the environment, pay and employment conditions. But the style of the leader – their communication and ability to connect – sets the context and establishes parameters for the overall employee experience and results.

An organisation might say they value collaboration or innovation; but if the leader is closed or has an outdated mindset, then we can wave goodbye to teamwork or innovative ideas. Employees emulate the behaviours of their leaders. So watch what you are modelling for your team.

Performance enhancers

Leaders can kill or ignite employee performance just by their leadership style and the way they interact with an individual or team. The communication style and impact of a leader determines their success and affects the entire organisation. Aligning their leadership style with the expectations and needs of employees is now a vital capability for leaders. Increasingly organisations are investing more time and energy in understanding their employees and creating great employee experiences by investing in new policies, programs and equipment to help turn work into a positive experience. However, I believe many of these initiatives only prop up failing cultures. Organisations can only truly enact the benefits of investment in employee experience initiatives if their leaders switch to a more inclusive style.

A great place to work includes a clearly defined strategy or purpose. It might have a leafy, air-conditioned office with paid days off for employees to support charities, flexible conditions, latest tech and other perks. But if the leadership doesn't connect or involve the team, and simply tells employees what to do, then those perks lose value. In this way, leader behaviour can drive down engagement despite the presence of extras or high wages. Leadership impact (*how* they communicate, make decisions and involve) is central to leveraging all other drivers of performance and engagement

– including employee conditions and privileges. Perks are designed to encourage and reward best performance, but that performance is limited by the leader's connection with the team.

Often in these scenarios, employee performance and engagement decline because workers realise that the perks are not reason enough to endure poor leadership or bad behaviour. There are two horizons to consider here.

In the short term, employees put up with a poor leader, enjoy the perks but resent not being involved or listened to. Ideas and change are negatively impacted, and employees consider other options in their future.

In the long term, employees decide the leader is not worth the perks or the hassle, and leave. Or in a worst-case scenario for the business, the employees might decide to stay, take the perks and reduce their work effort.

Either way, both horizons end badly for the business – all because of poor leadership style.

Activate joy at work

Organisations are investing in many programs to improve life at work; all focused on a better day-to-day experience for workers. While you can do much to improve factors such as employee work/life balance, recent research indicates the work itself is the most important.

When leaders make work meaningful for employees, it gives a sense of belonging, trust, and relationships. Perks are not the be-all and end-all of performance and engagement.

Joy is a powerful emotion that can enhance employees' performance and the success of the business. Leaders can improve joy at work by focusing conversations on employees' roles (harmony), how they contribute to goals (impact) and recognising their contribution (acknowledgement).

> ❝ Communication – the human connection – is the key to personal and career success. ❞
>
> *– Paul J. Meyer*

Conversations count

The more inclusive and more open you are as a leader, the greater your potential for creating impact and results. Conversations are like fertiliser, nourishing ideas and growing change across the business.

A culture where leaders commit to frequent two-way communication can fast track change, growth, innovation and safety. A culture of openness with a diversity of views or thought drives better results compared to cultures that do not communicate well. This is especially relevant when it comes to business transformation. When communication and conversation are embedded in the fabric of a business, they can adopt change and respond much more effectively.

When looking across industries, we see precisely the significance of leader communication impact on business cultures. Driving better safety and innovation is vital in healthcare and similar environments.

Take the following findings as evidence that the right conversations by open-minded leaders who communicate freely can leave a lasting legacy of results and change.

- Increased innovation, safer behaviours in operational environments
- Allow leaders to know what is happening across multiple levels and locations of the business
- Greater employee contribution to innovation and ideas
- Failure in communication can lead to death in places such as hospitals and transportation environments

Communication is necessary for organisational learning and growth, especially when it comes to complex and high-pressure environments.

More efficient operations

One aircraft maintenance company challenged its employees to find ways to better serve customers. Among the problems that surfaced was the difficulty of inspecting a particular aircraft part overnight. The inspection process typically took eight hours. The company's customers (airlines) found this frustrating because sometimes planes landed late and needed to take off early (Minor, et al., 2017).

As the service techs understood, the problem wasn't actually the inspection. It was the seven hour process of threading the camera inside the aircraft part to inspect it, when the subsequent inspection only took one hour.

An administrative assistant at the company who was familiar with the airlines' complaints, responded to the challenge. Having seen the Tom Cruise movie *Minority Report,* she posted an idea, wondering, 'Why can't we send a robotic spider into the part, like the ones in the movie?'

While many people reviewing her suggestion found it silly, the company's Chief Technology Officer was intrigued. He tried putting a miniature camera on a remote control set of robotic legs and walking it into the part. It worked. He turned the secretary's idea into standard practice. Now the inspections take 15 per cent of the time they used to, and the airlines are a lot happier.

This example teaches that involvement can have significantly more benefit and impact than hierarchy.

If you can't communicate, you can't lead

You might be wondering about the point of all this evidence that communication is so important? Well, leaders who invest time and energy building their communication capability get ahead and deliver better results because of their increased impact and influence. They achieve more than those with low communication capability. Put simply: if you can't communicate, you can't lead.

❛ I couldn't agree more with the premise of the vital importance of communication as part of leadership. I think the importance of engagement and connection for leaders is massively underestimated when you are dealing directly with people. ❜

– Michael Schneider, MD, Bunnings

Others agree too. More than 300,000 bosses, peers and teams were asked which skills have the greatest impact on a leader's success. Inspiring and motivating others (effective communication) was top. Other essential communication skills were also highly ranked as top leadership skills that are needed most. The findings add significant weight to the premise that if you can't communicate, then you really can't lead a team effectively, let alone an organisation (Minor, et al., 2017).

In an article for Gallup, Ryan Pendell described 'Eight Behaviors of the World's Best Managers'. These demonstrate the importance of a leader's impact and the way their communication sets the tone for company success. He writes that achieving a positive influence needs a leader to connect with the organisation strategy, build relationships with their team, listen and involve employees, set direction and lead in an open, empathic and honest manner. None of this is possible without communication capability and impact (Pendell, 2019).

Billionaire entrepreneur Richard Branson recognises its importance too, saying 'Communication is *the* most important skill any leader can possess' (Branson, 2015).

Communication impact activates the workforce and ensures that leaders can rally support for their vision and business effectively. Being able to communicate is a critical driver of leader success. I would say it's *the* most important skill a leader can have. If you have limited impact because you can't communicate, you get poor results.

Creating a following, building trust, engaging stakeholders, driving engagement, delivering results: all require effective communication. The ability to listen and enlist support is crucial. Don't get me wrong; there are leaders with substandard communication capability running teams and businesses. We have all worked with or for one (unfortunately). But the point is that those leaders would be significantly more successful and get better results if they increased their communication impact.

Telling and telepathy equals low impact

Five years ago, I worked with a senior executive who spent thousands of dollars developing an amazing business strategy – only to keep it hidden in the drawer, gathering dust. His approach was to tell employees what to do, on a need-to-know basis. Naturally, he was horrified when I suggested we provide the strategy to leaders to drive conversations with employees and customers. He was terrified that employees might find out where the business was heading commercially – or worse that they would tell the customers.

Ironically, this was the very thing employees needed to get involved and make the strategy a success. How could they innovate, change and improve if they didn't know the plan?

The leader's fear ensured that the entire workforce didn't know their future, resulting in lower employee engagement, unrest and insecurity. He was unable to activate support because he had not taken the time to connect and trust his employees. Hoping that employees might deliver because he asked them to was a great way to minimise impact and results.

(Of course, it might be news to some leaders that employees are not telepathic.)

Communication is a career-enhancing move

Perhaps most convincing to some, will be evidence from Korn Ferry that shows when leaders who are aspiring to be CEOs show communication capabilities, they dramatically raise the odds that they will become high performing chief executives. Communication impact can enhance your career chances (Lytkina Botelho, et al., 2017).

Activate the team

In an article in *HBR* magazine, Paul Zak wrote that 'Employees in high-trust companies are more productive, are more satisfied with their jobs, put in greater discretionary effort, are less likely to search for new jobs, and even are healthier than those working in low-trust companies' (Zak, 2019).

Four years ago, I worked in a major ASX firm that was struggling to reduce costs. One director decided to mandate a freeze on inter-state and international flights as an immediate cost-saving exercise. The decision came from him as an order, creating irritation and apathy among employees who resented the change. While costs came down in the short term, they eventually went back up when the travel ban was lifted.

At the same time, a different director enlisted the support of her team to develop cost-saving solutions. Involving and trusting employees in solving the problem brought a significant number of ideas that reduced costs. These included video conferencing, cheaper travel, different hotel suppliers and other sustainable changes aligned to business strategy.

These changes were owned by the employees and implemented effectively, producing a very different result with a productive and long-term outcome. The story highlights the need for leaders to balance the art of directing and involving to get the best results from their teams.

The impact of communication styles

Engagement requires leaders to pro-actively involve and include employees in decisions and projects. A balancing act of telling and asking will create optimal conditions that activate and inspire employees. Consider your leadership style against these four scenarios below. How balanced are you when it comes to leading and engaging?

Think about the degree of direction-setting and level of involvement your communication creates in your team or workforce.

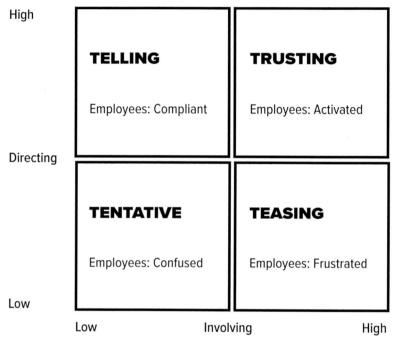

Figure 2: The four leader communicator types

Telling

In times of crisis, many leaders switch their communication style to telling to assert control. While this works in the short term, command and control or coercive leadership has been proven as the least effective of leadership styles for everyday business (Goleman, 2000). Author, Liz Ryan, suggests that telling is the leadership equivalent to a fax machine (Ryan, 2016). The 2020 workforce is educated and empowered. They expect leaders to listen and involve. Control and fear, caused by telling, de-humanises employees and shuts them down. Right now, employees and organisations need involvement and direction if they are to trust and support leaders.

Teasing

Spending too much time involving and consulting suggests that a leader can't decide. They appear to be teasing as they are seeking insight and ideas, but fail to take action. Leaders in this space mistake giving employees a voice (which creates trust) and instead give them a vote, which delays decisions and lacks direction. This creates inaction and misalignment, and erodes trust. Greater direction-setting by leaders will engage employees, driving up performance and trust.

> ❝ Effective communication is
> a way to success. ❞
> *– Jaspal Singh Malik*

Tentative

When leaders lack both direction and involvement, their communication is confusing and tentative. Instead of moving forward, they flip-flop on how to lead or engage and end up going nowhere. They confuse the team as they are unclear on vision and action. Increased direction and involvement in communication will grow trust and increase support.

Trusting

By setting a clear direction, involving your team in decisions, listening to their needs, empowering them to make decisions and solve problems, your communication style becomes trusting. It activates employees. They feel safe, take ownership, go the extra mile. As you practise traits that grow trust, you will continue to achieve more success.

Consider

Which style of leader communicator are you?

REFLECT

Five Takeaways:

- Leaders significantly influence the culture of the business
- If you can't communicate, you can't lead
- Perks or gimmicks are short-sighted
- Communication capability enhances your career
- Involvement activates employees.

Three Questions:

- What type of culture do I want to create?
- Am I balancing direction-setting and involvement?
- How am I going to move towards a more trusting communication style?

One Quote:

> ❝ Leadership has by far the largest and most direct effect on company culture. ❞
> — *William Craig, CEO and Founder of WebFX*

3

Price, Profit and Productivity

The cost of poor communication is often overlooked, underplayed or ignored by business. Many believe that improving communication is too hard or takes up too much money or time. This chapter shines a light on what is often regarded as unmeasurable. The numbers show that the business case for improving leader communication has never been stronger, more significant or straightforward than it is now.

When leaders get it right, there are many positive results — far more than I could list here. The ripple effect that runs through an organisation can yield a breathtaking impact. When a leader's communication doesn't hit the mark, the results can be just as far-reaching but in a very different or even disastrous way.

The price of poor communication

Do you have any idea how much leader communication is costing your business right now? I think you will be surprised at the amount of time, money and effort you could save. Small changes can yield a big collective difference.

Brace yourself – especially if you are a CEO, CFO or simply care about where the money goes in your organisation.

Australian businesses are a big player when it comes to low productivity. Research by Opinium, on behalf of Mitel, showed that most Australian employees consider as much as 14 per cent of their day is wasted because of poor communication. Their findings indicated that substandard communications cost organisations about $20,000 per employee every year. In an organisation with 1,000 people, that amounts to $20 million (Enterprise Agility, 2017). Yikes. Are you listening now?

Sure, managers are busy, with increasing workloads, and often quality conversations are not a priority. Thankfully just having a regular meeting with your team increases threefold the likelihood of employees being engaged. Yes, that's three times, not three per cent, and it's easily achievable.

Low employee engagement is one impact of poor communication with a perceived financial cost – and rightly so. In many operational businesses, it leads to a lack of innovation, low productivity, disruption, injuries or worse. Often companies are so used to poor communication or low innovation; they are unaware it exists. They believe it's just their culture or part of the way they work when actually they are caught up in a cycle of churn — going round and round doing the same thing and hoping for a different result. Usually, this is caused by leaders who don't communicate in ways that activate employees to change. Instead, they create apathy and compliance. Many teams are in a 'compliance coma'. They add significant cost to their organisation, just by existing. While this can create a financial burden, it is also a significant cause of poor employee wellbeing and poor mental health. It never ends well.

Some employees tire of poor culture or leadership and decide to leave, and this only increases when leaders don't listen or involve. Replacing employees who leave because they are uninspired or disengaged costs, and over time this can mount up to millions of dollars in a large business.

On the other side of the coin, engaged teams achieve greater productivity and better results. Leaders with engaged teams have more time to focus on their own goals and outcomes as their team is empowered and productive.

Productivity and profit

Higher engagement benefits the bottom line, reduces employee injuries and drives up productivity.

Many leaders fail to make the link between simple employee conversations and business results, instead, blaming employee attitude or apathy for poor outcomes. When engagement is high, leaders recognise that consistent and purposeful communication brings results across the board. Tony Johnson, CEO of EY, is one of those, writing that:

'The prize is substantial – a one per cent improvement in staff retention equates to a potential saving of $5.3 million annually that we can reinvest in growth' (Hastie, 2020).

A lack of internal communication is significantly impacting productivity and morale among employees, especially those in younger generations who want to be more involved or have their say. A report from The Economist Intelligence Unit, *Communication Barriers in the Workplace,* revealed that respondents believe communication barriers are leading to a delay or failure to complete projects (44 per cent), low morale (31 per cent), missed performance goals (25 per cent) and even lost sales (18 per cent). That same report indicated that 13 per cent of employees consider their organisations completely efficient in how they communicate and collaborate (The Economist Intelligence Unit, 2018).

❛ You cannot buy trust at any price. But slowly over time you can build it for free. ❜

– Jeffey Gitomer

Exercise: Run your numbers

Let's consider how much poor communication might be costing your organisation. Based on the research above, here's a quick scenario for an organisation with 1,000 employees.

Number of employees: 1,000

Cost per employee of poor communication: AU$20,000

Annual cost of poor communication: AU$20 million

So, how much is poor communication costing your business?

Use the following to help you calculate the cost of poor communication in your business or team.

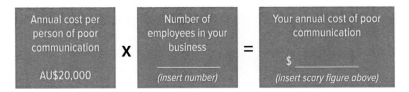

Figure 3: Calculating the cost of poor communication

This scenario presents a loud vote for improving communication and overall business performance. The numbers and the case for improving leader communication capability are strong. It stacks up and can turn around the fortunes of your company.

Investing in your leaders

Typically, the cost of improving leader communication capability starts at around $1,000 per person, per annum. Given the figures above, an investment of AU$50,000 in an organisation with fifty senior leaders, could drive a major return on effort year-on-year.

Investing $50,000 to save $20 million (cost of poor communication) seems like an easy decision to reach increased productivity, profit, innovation and more. You don't have to be a venture capitalist to recognise that investing in leader communication can profoundly impact your balance sheet and the organisation's fortunes.

The qualitative benefits of good leader communication are also significant.

Productive relations

Better employee relations are an outcome enjoyed by many operational leaders and businesses with good communication and high employee engagement. Leaders who build connections become more engaged themselves, as their teams are productive and successful, and ultimately make their leaders look good!

Labour, employee or industrial relations are significantly enhanced by regular, direct and productive conversations with employees. Trust in leaders, achieved through regular employee dialogue, plays a major part in this. Strikes, go-slows, planned sickness and other industrial sabotage, can be reduced or avoided with regular dialogue.

Better results for managers

Managers who communicate effectively make a greater contribution to business results by having engaged teams. They create opportunities for success, enabling more ideas, effort and impact from their teams.

The engaged leader has more time to think, plan and succeed, as they no longer feel the need to solve every problem. Their team resolves issues, takes ownership, creates more solutions and experiences fewer issues.

But wait, there's more...

Consider these additional metrics and numbers when adding up the cost of poor communication and low employee engagement communication to your business.

A 2017 Gallup report on the state of the global workforce showed that workgroups with high levels of employee engagement experience 17 per cent higher productivity, 59 per cent lower turnover, 10 per cent higher customer ratings and 20 per cent higher sales.

Additionally, the report indicated that

- Engaged workforces have 70 per cent fewer safety incidents.
- Replacing an employee who leaves because a leader doesn't listen or engage, costs 2.5 times their salary.

- Organisations in the bottom quartile of engagement scores experience 41 per cent higher turnover. Those with good communication have up to 65 per cent lower turnover.

- Good communication and high employee engagement can result in some or all of these:

  » Workgroups with high engagement have 21 per cent higher profits.

  » Companies with high engagement earn 2.6 times higher per share levels than low engagement companies.

  » High engagement is recognised as adding 10 per cent to customer ratings (Gallup, 2017).

Are you convinced yet?

REFLECT

Five Takeaways:

- The quality of your communication can cost or benefit your business
- Poor communication costs AU$20,000 per employee per year
- Good communication creates more profit and value
- The business case for improving communication is strong
- The quality of your communication can influence your career.

Three Questions:

- How much is poor communication costing your organisation?
- What benefits could you see from better communication?
- How much easier would your work be with conversations and communication embedded in your day-to-day leadership?

One Quote:

❝ No matter how you slice it, effective communication is key to team and organizational success. ❞
— *Michael Schneider, Welltower*

4

Climbing the Ladder of Impact

Communication, like leadership, is a skill in which we invest time and energy to ensure we improve or maintain our capability. Leaders who thrive, commit to continuous learning and improvement. They reflect and take on feedback to ensure they can grow and adapt to changes. They try new ways to achieve outcomes and consistently ask, 'How can I get better?'

This chapter looks at how leaders can improve and climb the ladder of communication impact to improve engagement and trust, as that is ultimately what creates and drives outcomes. Each rung of the ladder depicts a level of leadership communication capability, impact and trust built with employees.

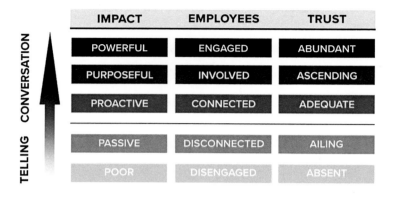

Figure 4: Powerful communication ladder of impact

❝ We need to create an epiphany moment, so leaders understand the importance of having conversations instead of telling. This is partly about rewarding and recognising the right behaviours in leaders. But say, for example, I was working with an executive who is high on telling, sometimes you have to make them aware. Show them where they are and in which paradigm they are operating and explain the impacts that can have on people or outcomes. ❞

– Michael Schneider, MD, Bunnings

The ladder of impact

When leaders communicate and have conversations, they create an impact. The scale and nature of vary according to their ability to communicate. In turn, this affects their results and the degree of trust and engagement created with employees. As mentioned in earlier chapters, your ability to communicate either lifts or limits your results.

Leaders who sit at the top of the ladder have invested time and effort in building their leadership and communication capability. The ladder illustrates how personal capability improves results and grows more positive outcomes.

Let's start with the lowest rung.

Poor communicators

We've already seen how poor communication yields disengaged employees and low results. Leaders with these limited capabilities generally don't know how to do better. They often come from the command and control school of leadership, which doesn't value conversation or listening. That means they are focused on their way of doing things and less concerned with the involvement and ideas of others. Perhaps they value their own ideas more than those of their team. In this sense, they are not aligned to their workforce as they are telling, not building conversations.

These leaders don't create the right energy, so their employees are unmotivated, disconnected or change-resistant. Instead of planning communication in the form of regular team meetings, the leaders avoid them. Listening and involvement are considered a waste of time. Poor communicators who are focused on telling, don't want to hear others' opinions. They might think they have all the answers but are operating in an old fashioned style of leadership.

A lack of engagement can cause problems for customers, with errors, poor alignment, incidents/injuries and complaints. Friction with other teams arises with lack of collaboration, clarity and poor performance. Without direction, the team will likely be marginalised.

A reputation for poor communication often sits alongside low emotional intelligence resulting in blunt, ill-considered or poorly timed conversations. There is significant scope to increase employee trust and impact for this leader.

Traits of poor communicators

- Mindset: 'I say, you do'
- Key channel used: Orders
- Focus: Micromanagement and telling
- Cause of failure: Control, power, authority.

Passive communicators

With disconnected employees and below average results, these leaders rely on others or systems to communicate for them. They are inactive as they see communication as an optional extra to their job as a manager.

Passive leaders rely on the organisation's traditional 'cascade system' to receive and pass on messages in a one-way, antiquated style of leadership. Email is often their primary tool, with no real thought for the needs of their audience.

They avoid feedback and important conversations. Passive leaders often hide from face-to-face communication as they lack the confidence and conviction to go outside their comfort zone. They want to fly under the radar without having to put themselves 'out there' in the business.

Not known for living the organisation's values, they are most often in their office with the door closed (sending emails!). These leaders 'tick and flick' to ensure compliance and don't welcome ideas or feedback. Conversations with the team are few and far between as their relationship is apathetic and disconnected.

Engagement is not a priority for this leader. They lack visibility and don't give candid feedback. Unable to prioritise communication or build enthusiasm for change in others, they might be overwhelmed. More regular communication by a passive leader could alleviate team friction, increase collaboration with others and reduce anxiety about roles and contribution in the team. They are capable of much more with the right focus and effort.

By having a regular team meeting and connecting more regularly with employees, they are three times more likely to have engaged employees. This would create positive impacts on their results and move them above the line from passive to proactive.

Traits of passive communicators

- Mindset: 'Communication is an optional extra
- Key channel used: Telepathy or the cascade
- Focus: Compliance and hierarchy
- Cause of failure: Apathy and low trust from others.

Proactive communicators

These usually visible leaders have some communication rhythms in place to reach their people. Team members are connected to their work but not emotionally or mentally plugged in – mainly because the leader is inconsistent or over-communicates. When the leader does communicate, they are over-confident, unfocused or make it all about them, not their audience. They can appear narcissistic and are often highly technical experts with the 'curse of confidence'.

This leader lacks the real commitment to communication that would boost trust and encourage employees to consistently go above and beyond. By being more visible, connected and committed, the leader sets a stronger example and creates a safer space for others to be proactive. Instead, they are hot and cold communicators – inconsistent, despite being proactive. Their lack of commitment impacts their team. Because they are not focused on their communication, the team is not focused on their results. Switching back and forth between telling and conversation creates a lack of trust in some employees.

The most significant change the proactive leader can make is to focus. Making communication about the role and contribution of the team will help them see how they fit into the big picture. With focus and consistency, the leader will grow a deeper connection and build trust with their team.

There is significant room to raise engagement on this rung of the ladder, using targeted and regular employee involvement, and dialogue that is aligned to the audience, not the leader!

Traits of proactive communicators

- Mindset: 'I've got this'
- Key channel used: Anything that comes to mind
- Focus: Me! Me! Me!
- Cause of failure: Winging it. Overconfidence. Inconsistency.

Purposeful communicators

These leaders prioritise communication. They are visible and connected to both the team and the organisation. Leaders at this level involve employees, but might not set a clear direction or consistently connect team involvement to the bigger picture. They assume that involvement is the same as engagement, sometimes failing to 'land the plane' when it comes to decision-making. They can mistake giving employees a voice for giving them a vote.

To go beyond involvement and secure more effort from employees, progressing leaders need to focus on the purpose of their communication and build a deeper connection with their team. They would benefit from a communication rhythm that is established and precise, and from identifying the purpose of each communication channel.

Thinking about the desired outcome of every communication will help build purpose, channelling employee energy and ideas onto the areas most needed by the business. One simple tactic is to include a clear call to action in every communication. This can take the audience from informed to engaged and trusting because they are invited to follow through and encouraged to play their part consistently. However, results rely on the leader following up on actions and holding employees to account, which will also create more trust.

Traits of purposeful communicators

- Mindset: 'Ask the audience'
- Key channel used: Ears
- Focus: Involving others
- Cause of failure: Doesn't land on decisions, too busy listening.

Powerful communicators

These leaders host regular two-way conversations, building a solid connection with their teams based on abundant trust. That means they are highly visible. They understand and consider the challenges employees face. Each communication is purposeful and aligned to business goals and outcomes.

Engagement is high in their teams, and so results are consistent and positive. Leaders at this level invest time connecting employees to vision and goals. They unite their team and translate strategic themes or priorities into actions and outputs.

Powerful communication means these leaders have open and honest conversations. They recognise and reward others and have challenging conversations because they are trusted and see the value in feedback for and from others. They use logic to help explain their decisions and demonstrate that they care for their team.

Powerful communicators also reflect on their capability and continually improve. Understanding the needs and preferences of a changing workforce, they are high on the scale of emotional intelligence and connection.

Traits of powerful communicators

- Mindset: 'Communication is how I lead/enable others to succeed'
- Key channel used: Whatever fits the audience
- Focus: Empower others to deliver results
- Cause of failure: Lack of direction from their leader could demotivate them.

❝ If a leader can explain their strategy and rationale for decisions, then the outcome is that people will feel like they are involved in the journey and are more likely to trust. They don't necessarily have to agree with you, they just have to understand where you are coming from. Once you achieve that, you can progress your agenda and do it in a way where people will trust you and respect you. ❞

– Michael Schneider, MD, Bunnings

Exercise: Find your rung

Before we move into *how* to improve communication capability, let's set a benchmark for where you or your leaders are now. This will help you build on existing skills and reflect on improvement.

Having read this chapter, where are you on the communication impact ladder?

Which aspects of your communication and leadership can you improve? (Keep these in mind for the next section of this book.)

How can you start to focus more on conversation and less on telling? Every leader can improve on this.

What are your team or unit engagement scores? Have them ready so you can reflect over the next few chapters.

How do you feel about changing your style of leadership and communication? Keeping a positive and open mind will help you learn how to have and host powerful conversations.

The perception gap

Perceptions of the same experience often vary widely. At work, a leader might think they have communicated effectively, thoroughly and with impact, while employees or customers feel they are still in the dark, have half the story or lack key information.

As George Bernard Shaw is often quoted: 'The single greatest problem in communication is the illusion that it has taken place.'

Perception (and the potential fall out of differing perceptions) is why leaders need to be intentional and deliberate about communicating with their teams. Viewing communication as optional pushes it down the list of priorities and creates scenarios where it might not happen. Remember the $20 million?

Some years ago, I worked with a large business that had decided to outsource 400 employees in a move to reduce costs and focus on core customer offerings. They decided to pay another provider to maintain their assets rather than run those services themselves. Nothing unusual about that, I agree.

High risk/high rewards projects like these need strong and effective two-way dialogue to ensure smooth delivery. The workers being outsourced were union aligned, blue-collar workers, so, the risk of disruption to services, negative media or poor engagement was high. Communication depended on good conversations, not telling, and the workers expected to have their say.

I surveyed the leaders asking how effective they thought they were in their communication capability. Ninety-seven per cent rated themselves as good or excellent – an amazing and confident result.

At the same time, I asked the employees for feedback on their leaders' communication. The result was very different. Employees said they rarely heard or saw their leaders — and when they did connect, it was unsatisfactory or negative.

Unfortunately, such results are not unique to this organisation. Leaders' perceptions that they have communicated and connected can be in total contrast with their teams. There was, in this example, a significant gap between the leaders' perception of how good they were and their actual behaviour or capability.

It was time for a reality check.

I presented the results to the leadership team and recommended lifting communication capability as our first action. This proved a tipping point for the project as the leaders saw the perception gap as a call to arms. The risk of unsatisfactory results from poor leader communication created a platform for me to work with the leaders and help them improve. The outcome was better stakeholder engagement and better leadership. Industrial action was avoided, and unit performance increased so much that outsourcing was eventually put aside.

Leaders can't outsource their communication

Often leaders ask me to make them look good. Improving their communication capability is the most effective way to do this. That way they *are* genuinely better, not just appearing so.

Communication competence ensures that leaders understand how to communicate. After all, as the face of the organisation, both internally and externally, they cannot outsource their communication or personal brand building to others. To succeed, they must demonstrate that they understand their audience, show they can listen, have emotional intelligence and can make decisions and create support for them.

Each leader has individual strengths when it comes to engaging stakeholders. But to improve any leader's performance or impact, they need honest feedback on how they are perceived.

In this sense, leaders need to mind the gap between how they think they are perceived (self-view) and how their audience perceives them (their brand). I have worked with many leaders providing this feedback and supporting an uplift of communication capability. The ladder of capability that helps leaders climb from poor to powerful communication has come from this work.

The curse of confidence

Leaders are often experts in their field or have worked in their sector for decades. So why would they be anything other than confident when addressing an audience or customer? Yet too often, I see self-assured leaders address stakeholders or hold a difficult conversation without preparation. Here, confidence alone can be a curse that leads to poor outcomes. There are several facets to communication capability, and confidence is only one.

I once worked with a leader who made stuff up on the spot when presenting to employees. He was a people pleaser. In many ways, his communication capability was good as he was engaging, funny, and informed. But he was not aligned to what the audience needed.

He told them what he thought they wanted to hear, gave away secrets and made announcements that were not agreed or approved. Over time his employees became so used to his over-promises that they stopped believing him and stopped listening. He spent lots of time rethinking decisions he had shared prematurely, or retrofitting his words to align with reality. His curse of confidence undermined trust and damaged his reputation.

I challenge leaders to reflect on their communication efforts and to seek honest feedback from their teams, customers and others. Audience response is a gift that helps them to build more impact or capability and, in turn, become better leaders.

REFLECT

Five Takeaways:

- Telling limits
- Conversations lift
- Involvement creates impact
- Impact builds trust
- Trust yields results.

Three Questions:

- Where are you on the ladder of impact?
- What would improve for you as you move upwards?
- What might be business-wide results if you and your peers moved upwards?

One Quote:

> ❝ Your ability to communicate either lifts or limits your results. ❞
>
> *– Paul Matthews*

Warning!

You're about to read Part Two, that will help you to create significantly better outcomes. If you allow, it will activate your engagement super-powers, tap into a powerful network of support and lift the ceiling on your results. Are you ready?

PART

2

Let's Switch

The second half of this book provides a highly practical and relevant step-by-step process to guide leaders and organisations up the capability ladder towards more powerful communication.

As leaders, we are already busy with lots to deliver, so the last thing we need is more work. Powerful communication yields trusting conversations and can help you get better results from your workforce without extra burden.

Chapter Five introduces the Powerful Conversation model, which is unpacked in the following chapters.

Chapter Six unpacks the *why* of your communication improvement and shows how a change in mindset and thinking can influence your results.

Chapter Seven is where we build a plan to listen and get close to our team. This helps us understand the *who* in our communication.

Chapter Eight outlines how we can focus on the right areas — otherwise known as the *what* of communication.

And finally, **Chapter Nine** is where we prioritise the frequency of conversations, their rationale and purpose. This phase focuses on *how* we lead and sustain important and powerful conversations.

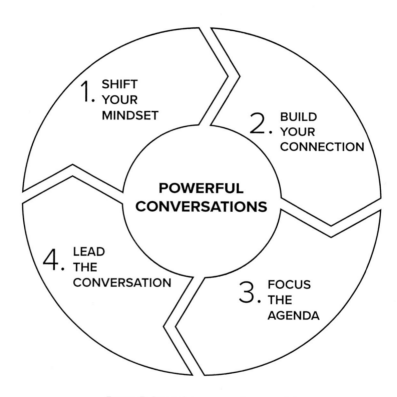

Figure 5: Powerful conversations model

5

Four Steps to Powerful Conversations

Powerful conversations are a way of leading that engage the workforce more effectively and with ease. They are specifically designed to help leaders connect and build great trust.

Powerful conversations are *how* you engage and lead, not an additional activity on your to-do list. By embedding these conversations in your day-to-day work, you will eventually reduce the amount of effort and time that communication currently takes up. Let's explore each part of the powerful conversations approach and then look at how to embed it.

A model for powerful conversations

This model of improvement uses a combination of mental and environmental adjustments for leaders and teams to build trust. It considers you and others in your setting. The process is circular and based on a process of continual learning and improvement. Similar to the traditional Plan-Do-Check-Act model devised by William Denning, it is easy to use. Let's take a look.

Shift your Mindset: the WHY

This first phase asks you to consider the *why* of your communication improvement. Here we'll look at how a change in mindset and thinking can influence your results. This will help you to try different approaches, feel less cynical about others and not take things personally when they go wrong.

You might uncover reasons for your lack of improvement or why something might push you forward. This phase helps you stay open to opportunities ahead. We'll explore the personal benefits to you.

> ❝ The art of communication is the
> language of leadership. ❞
> – *James Humes*

Build Your Connection: the WHO

We cannot understand what our audience wants or needs unless we are connected with them. Many businesses spend millions of dollars on market research and customer analysis, but as leaders, we need to invest time and energy getting under the skin of our employees to build an emotional connection to use in our communication. The premise of this section is that the workforce has evolved, and if we are to succeed, so must we. We have to understand our employees and our audience to do that.

Here we build a plan to listen and get close to our team, helping us understand the who in our communication.

Focus the Agenda: the WHAT

In his book of the same name, Daniel Goleman defines focus as the hidden driver of excellence (Goleman, 2013). This is no different when it comes to communication and getting results. Chapter Eight outlines how we can focus on the right areas — otherwise known as the *what* of communication. This phase enables you to connect employees to their roles, to team goals and business strategy.

Here we build the content or the agenda for our conversations, helping us understand what we are going to communicate on any given occasion.

Lead the conversation: the HOW

Chapter Nine helps you to build the right infrastructure, systems and platforms for an ongoing two-way conversation, based on the learning from previous phases. Our conversations will take place in a number of forums and on different platforms, face-to-face or through technology. Having and choosing the right channel and timing is critical, as we will soon discover.

This is where we prioritise the frequency of conversations, their rationale and purpose. This phase focuses on how we lead and sustain important and powerful conversations.

> ❝ Communication is a skill that you can learn.
> It's like riding a bicycle or typing. If you're
> willing to work at it, you can rapidly improve
> the quality of every part of your life. ❞
> *– Brian Tracy*

Learning along the way

As we move, apply and work through the Powerful Conversations approach, we build learning and outcomes along the way. These are valuable as they help us consider our actions, understand the importance of our conversations and apply these learnings. Insights, alignment, clarity and results are significant outcomes that will lead us to bigger results and more trust.

Insights

Investing time in understanding our employees is invaluable. These insights frame our behaviours and discussion. They help us build an emotional connection so we can read people better. The insights create a mental profile of individuals and teams, so we know what will hit the mark when communicating. It enables us to give employees what they need because we 'get' them.

Alignment

Once we've built a connection with the team and focused our agenda effectively, we create alignment as our communication matches the needs of the team and organisation. Knowing their preferences informs our approach. With clear and accurate communication, employees get what they want, and results are delivered.

Clarity

Clarity comes from focusing our communication agenda and having a conversation with our team. If we are all on the same page, then we can move forward together towards our goals effectively. Clarity is vital – if there is none, then communication fails and results suffer.

Results

At the end of this process, we will have opened our minds, connected with the team, built a clear agenda and held a productive conversation, creating results with individual employees and the team. Once we commit to shifting our mindset and passing through each phase, we deliver on our outcomes. Communication is all about results. If we don't have an end in mind, then we can't start. Let's not confuse powerful conversations with chit-chat. After all, this is all about improving your leadership and your team's performance.

REFLECT

Five Takeaways:

- Focus on your impact
- Improve over time
- No one is perfect
- Make a plan
- You've got this!

Three Questions:

- What is your ultimate goal for improving your communication?
- What role can your leader play in this?
- How can others in the organisation help you?

One Quote:

> ❝ A goal without a plan is just a wish. ❞
> — *Antoine de Saint-Exupéry*

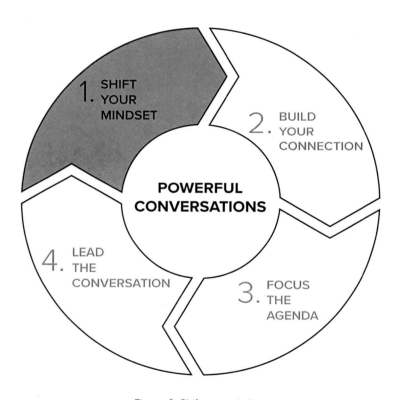

Figure 6: Shift your mindset

6

Shift Your Mindset

My mindset has helped me advance and grow, and I would argue that yours too dictates your success. So much so, that I believe everyone can become a powerful communicator, trusted and influential in their leadership. With the right focus, effort and growth, we can all connect with our audience and lead powerful conversations. I wrote this book so every leader can challenge themselves to improve their communication and therefore be a better leader.

Are you open to change?

Successful leaders and good communicators are more likely to have a growth mindset. By this, I mean they are open to new ways of doing things because they believe they can learn new skills and perform existing ones to a higher level. They value support and advice, seeing challenges, obstacles and feedback as an opportunity to improve and grow.

If you believe you can be a great and powerful communicator, you are more likely to make that happen. That is because you have a growth mindset that encourages you to improve. It helps you improve, learn and achieve more and easier.

If, on the other hand, you think you already have all the answers or tell yourself that you can't improve your results, then you probably won't. Your fixed mindset allows limited results, and you are unlikely to change with that attitude and self-talk.

Let's face it: none of us is perfect. We can all improve, so being closed to improvement is limiting our lives and successes. It's not hard to grasp when we think of it this way.

Switching your mindset to be positive and open to change and improvement is a major part of powerful conversations. That is why the mindset shift is at the start of the powerful conversations journey so that leaders can create belief early on.

Let's explore the impact your thoughts can have on your leadership and communication results. Start by telling yourself that it is time to look beyond your old or existing ways and that trying something new might be exciting and helpful.

Your mindset = your success

The first step towards powerful communication involves switching our mindset to believe we can get better results using conversations and trust. You must believe you can be a great or better communicator by involving others and listening more. Loosening control and letting go of any desire to tell people what to do is a key part of this. Once you accept that you can lead with conversations and get better results, you are much more likely to do so.

Focus on your mindset

Mindset is an inner voice that can predict your success as a communicator and leader, by lifting you up or bringing you down. Carol Dweck of Stanford University is an authority on mindset. She sees mindset as a major decider of success and learning where a growth mindset enables you to 'see challenges as exciting rather than limiting'. She believes, as do I, that with the right mindset and the right teaching people are capable of a lot more than we think. This is why I believe we can all be powerful communicators. If you have a fixed mindset, you may see failures or setbacks as evidence that you're not good enough. And you know what happens to most people when they hear that? They get stuck. And they don't try anymore (Mindvalley, 2019).

The right mindset means choosing growth and improvement over negative self-talk and self-imposed limitations to potential. Instead of agreeing that they aren't good enough, people with a growth mindset decide to push back. They tell themselves that they may not have the ability to do it now. But they can change that.

Keep telling yourself *you can* until those thoughts become a habit, and eventually, you'll see those fixed mindset statements melt away.

FIXED MINDSET

GROWTH MINDSET

'Seeing failure as evidence that you are not good enough.'

'Telling yourself that you can.'

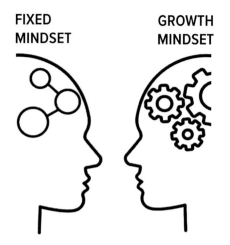

Figure 7: Growth and fixed mindset

Features of a fixed mindset

If you have a fixed mindset, you might tell yourself some of these:

- I'm not a natural communicator
- Telling is better than conversations
- I'm not charismatic, so I can't engage
- I'm more of a listener than a speaker
- Communication is not part of my job
- Employees aren't listening to me
- Employees don't do as they are told.
- My engagement scores won't shift.

The reality is that all of these statements can be proved wrong. Every leader has the ability to lift their communication effectiveness and results. This involves switching our mindset, framing our inner talk in more positive language and motivating ourselves to try different strategies to create change. I know it works, as I have seen it happen.

Some leaders might tell themselves that they are 'operations' or 'technology' leaders. They might think that they don't need to inspire, unite or build trust. These are fixed mindset stories because they haven't accepted the importance of communication in success. Every leader, no matter what stage in their career or sector they work in, will benefit from more powerful and trusting conversations.

A national Australian logistics company I worked with was male-dominated and had a change-resistant culture. The workforce was highly unionised with low trust in management. My role was to help middle managers improve employee engagement. One leader lacked confidence, saying he was 'no good at comms'. He believed 'employees just want to be told what to do', as this removed any doubt or questions.

At the same time, team safety and productivity were poor. The first challenge to improving the Supervisor's results was to silence his inner voice. We worked on creating the belief that he was a good communicator and that when employees ask questions, this cements their understanding and commitment further. He eventually accepted that he could get better, witnessing a change in the team and more positive results as his mindset shifted from fixed to growth. This became a cycle of belief, confidence and growth.

Features of a growth mindset

If you have a growth mindset, you might tell yourself some of these:

- I can learn how to be a better communicator
- I can ask for feedback to help me grow
- I can build confidence
- I can be engaging in my own way
- I am going to embrace communication as a part of my job
- I am getting better each time I do this
- I can grow my results if I increase my impact and effort
- I am getting better every day.

A growth mindset creates energy and motivation to get better and move forward.

I talked with John Banfield, the CEO of BPAY, about mindset. Here are his thoughts.

'MAD: Make A Difference. I talk about this all the time and use examples of how I and others have or could make a difference for employees or customers. MAD is based on the saying that happy employees make happy customers. My mindset is that I want to empower my team. I want to ensure I have a great set of people, walking side by side with me in the trenches. Side by side that is, not hiding behind me. I want them to fulfil the company ambition and their own and be accountable and responsible.'

Switching your mindset

There are many ways to build a growth mindset – here are some suggestions. Remember that leaders with a growth mindset think differently. They learn to take lessons from errors or mistakes and see them as learning experiences. Many leaders consider that unless you are failing, you cannot be learning.

Five steps to a growth mindset

1. *Commit to learning*

   Commit to learning from things that go wrong or don't work. Every leader has failed. It is said that those who fail most, achieve most. Failure just means you can try something different next time, and it's statistically more likely to work. Tell yourself you don't need to waste your time doing the same thing again because you recognise it didn't get the outcome you wanted. The best way to get things right is to spend time getting them wrong. Getting used to failure makes it easier to process and move on to success.

2. *Surround yourself with people who inspire you*

   Spending time with people you admire immerses you in new ways and new ideas. Conversations with those who are doing things differently will help you build the courage and energy to try new things and achieve a different outcome yourself.

   The more time you spend with others who are doing what you want to do, the more likely you are to experiment and learn from them. Their example reinforces that it's safe to try something different.

3. *Find tools to help you try new things*

The Internet is packed with ideas of new or different ways of doing things. Run a Google search for 'Improving team meetings', and you'll find around 220 million results in under a second. That's because so many other people have already done the work for you. Try some of them out — and if they don't work, try a different one next time.

4. *Plan*

Make a plan to guide your communication progress. This will help you get better incrementally without being overwhelmed or defeated. A plan will hold you accountable, motivate and reward your progress. The next few chapters of this book lay out a blueprint of suggested improvements for you. Follow them to build your personalised plan for having powerful leadership conversations.

5. *Share if you care*

When mentoring leaders, I always start our first session by sharing these two statements.

1. If you write down a plan, you are already 40 per cent likely to achieve it. These are good, but not great, odds.

2. If you write down a plan and share it with someone you respect or admire, then you are 70 per cent likely to achieve it. These are much better odds.

My recommendation is that you write a plan and share it with your manager, another leader or your mentor if you have one. Or send it to me at paul@commscoach.org, and I promise to check in on your progress.

> ❝ Successful outcomes are never the result of a single choice. They are built up through good choices over time. A profitable business is never a choice, it is a series of choices. A fit body is never a choice, it is a series of choices. A strong relationship is never a choice, it is a series of choices. ❞
> – *James Clear*

Think of your goal as moving up the steps of the powerful communication ladder in Chapter Four. Consider each action you take as enabling you to get better and closer to being a more successful leader and more powerful communicator. Break down the actions outlined in the following pages and be deliberate about your growth. Move through each chapter with purpose and apply the changes as you move forward. Don't try to do everything at once or you will feel inundated. Focus on doing a few things well, not lots of things perfectly or all at once.

Below is a smaller scale example of ways to improve your team meetings. This is a real example used by a leader in government who wanted to create more regular, focused team discussions.

OUTCOME: More regular, focused and productive team discussions.	
Goal	**Action**
Get more feedback	Each month ask, 'What should I start, stop or keep doing?'
Get more ideas	Hold a HOW conversation (see later) at each meeting
Align discussion to goals	Align the meeting agenda to business objectives or plans
Target team discussion	Agree on the agenda before the meeting and stick to it
More two-way discussion	Arrange a monthly meeting and invite team members.

Table 2: Improving team meetings

REFLECT

Five Takeaways:

- Be open
- Think positively
- Try new things
- Find new ways
- Learn from mistakes.

Three Questions:

- How will you practise being open to change and improvement?
- Who might be a good mentor or someone you can learn from?
- Who or what is stopping you from growing and learning?

One Quote:

❝ Just because some people can do something with little or no training, it doesn't mean that others can't do it (and sometimes do it even better) with training. ❞
— *Carol Dweck*

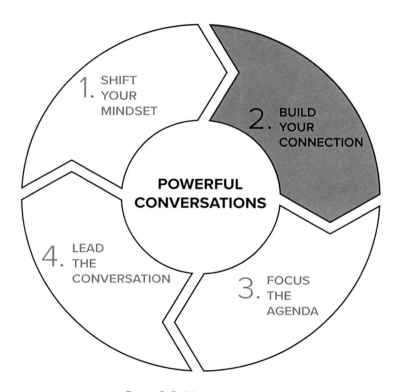

Figure 8: Build your connection

7

Build Your Connection

I know *connection* feels like a current corporate buzzword, but it's just a way to describe the bond between leaders and employees. It's an important focus because the connection you build with your team determines the degree of trust, and that, in turn, defines your success. No tricks or tools are necessary — leaders already have all the magic they need to build strong and productive connections with employees.

Your communication and engagement super-powers already exist inside you. They are there for the taking. Once activated, you will be able to ignite employee effort and build trust with ease.

This chapter explores the second aspect of powerful conversations: building your connection. It explores the simple yet sophisticated ways leaders can establish and improve this priceless bond — just by being themselves.

> If you have trust, then you can build a team. Achievement flows from that. Teams might not always win, for example, as being the most profitable, but they will win through being more engaged and connected. That leads to innovation and growth.
>
> — *Michael Schneider, MD, Bunnings*

Whether you're leading in retail, financial services, tech or construction, the connection with your employees could just be your most prized asset. If you only invest in one part of the powerful communication model, then this is it! Why? Deeper connection makes the whole business of leadership so much easier.

Why connect?

Many leaders still ask, 'What is meant by connection?' Managers who spend time learning about their employees understand them better, with a deeper appreciation of them as individuals and as colleagues. They know them on many levels and are therefore more connected to them. This builds the leader's confidence and courage to communicate more effectively. Connection helps leaders have difficult conversations, correct or discuss performance and behaviour. Connected leaders can ask for more from employees, but they often get more without having to ask!

A deeper connection with your employees makes your leadership and communication more effective because it is aligned or targeted to employee needs. When we understand our employees, we connect to them on an emotional level. Being human and showing that you are the same as others increases results and boosts trust. Employees let down their guard, open up and let you in when they see you are like them.

Remember that connection cuts both ways. First and foremost, it bolsters trust in you as a leader, and it also enables you to trust your employees to do more. This means you can ask for more, expect more, achieve more and ultimately let go of work that your team can deliver without close supervision.

So much has been written about connection and emotional intelligence over recent years. It is now accepted and proved that EQ helps leaders get improved results. We know that businesses in all industries are more successful when their leaders display EQ. The main reason for this is that these leaders understand their employees and apply this when they make decisions or communicate. Their ability to unite and motivate a workforce is amplified with EQ.

❝ Be human. Show the real person inside so that employees connect with you. It's amazing what that does to open up a conversation. Being passionate is the best thing you can ever do for yourself. Others will connect with you far easier than they ever have after they see your vulnerabilities. ❞
– John Banfield CEO, BPAY

Your six super-powers

In a recent article, Daniel Goleman, a global authority on leadership and emotional intelligence, wrote, 'Technical skills and self-mastery alone allow you to be an outstanding individual contributor. But to lead, you need an additional interpersonal skill set: you've got to listen, communicate, persuade, collaborate' (Goleman, 2011).

You don't need to put on a disguise and go on Undercover Boss to get to know your team. Every leader has a set of connection super-powers they can use to learn about their team. These enable leaders to fast track connection by understanding employees more. They help build trust and impact. The good news is you already have these powers and are most likely using them, but not at work and not in this way.

The following Six Connection Super-Powers use senses and abilities that you already have. They are the keys to powerful conversations:

- **Feeling:** imagine how employees feel and the reasons for this
- **Listening**: seek employee views, feedback and ideas
- **Thinking:** consider what information employees need to succeed
- **Giving:** provide employee feedback, recognition and be generous with your time

- **Tasting:** get close to employees, sample their world
- **Speaking:** explain the direction and needs of the business.

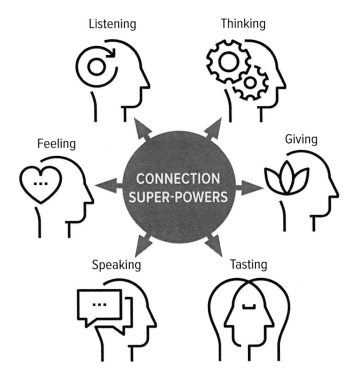

Figure 9: Connection super-powers

Collectively these powers will provide priceless insights into your team. They allow you to get ahead. Using these skills helps build trust fast, making your impact and results much more powerful. With some self-reflection and commitment to change, every leader can improve their insights using their super-powers.

Super-powers will help grow your EQ. By spending more time with employees, leaders grow to understand and recognise their emotional state. This is vital, as emotions convey information, prompts and clues about what is going on in a team or business. Don't just take my word for it. Daniel Goleman says, 'Above all, engagement comes down to human connection,' which is why using your super-powers really matters. Empathetic leaders communicate better when they can read the emotional landscape of their team. They listen and understand employees. The insights they gain increase the impact of their communication, cranking up team productivity.

> ❝ Emotional intelligence is important at work. We need to be able to communicate intuitively, for example, I might say to a team: 'I can't read your mind, but I can read your body language. As leaders, we need to be able to sense when we are or are not hitting the mark with our leadership or communication. We need to consider the psychology of the team or organisation. ❞
> – *Bronwyn Evans, CEO, Engineers Australia*

Empathy plays a key role in the retention and motivation of employees. Leaders have always needed empathy to develop and keep good people, but today in the evolved workplace, the stakes are much higher (Goleman, 2004).

Lessons from an eight-year-old

A few years ago, I looked after my eight-year-old niece for the day. My family said she was an 'easy child'. 'No trouble,' they said. I hadn't spent much time with her, so I didn't know her preferences. I couldn't predict her responses. I even offered lollies and a trip to the movies to get her to go along with my plans for the day. It bombed, and she refused to go. I should have invested more time asking what she wanted to do and listening to her. Then I would have known that she was (and still is) fanatical about being at the stables, mucking out and spending time with horses – not going to the movies.

Connection during crisis

Gladys Berejiklian and Daniel Andrews, Premiers of NSW and Victoria respectively, were recently front and centre helping lead state-based responses to the devastating bush fires in Australia. They attended many local communities spending time with firefighters and those impacted by the crises. They did so just like other political leaders, but with limited publicity. Berejiklian was praised for her swift action and for taking time to visit the devastation. She was clearly moved by it personally, too.

Andrews was also highly invested in ensuring the state recovered safely. He too was praised for his honesty, action and consideration of the situation and the struggle his state faced. Their immersion in the crises, connection with the community and understanding of the impact were significant factors in the way they lead their responses. Berejiklian empathised with those impacted. She felt their pain. She understood what was happening and the severity of the fires. Irrespective of her politics, the locals valued her visit, her listening and her presence.

Compare this response with Scott Morrison, Prime Minister of Australia, who also undertook a tour of bush fire-ravaged areas. He spent time trying to connect with the community but appeared to use the situation to his advantage, inviting media and promoting his leadership and party. It backfired. The media bashed him for 'fake condolences and forced handshakes as the nation burned'. He made matters worse by then going on holiday to Hawaii, before a slow and inadequate response to the fires. The latter proved he was not connected or invested as much as he should have been. He was out of touch with the community, and so was his leadership and communication. He lacked an emotional connection with those impacted. Not surprisingly this all ended badly for the Prime Minister. Locals refused to shake his hand because of his lack of leadership and empathy with their situation. Ouch!

The root cause of the PM's downfall was his lack of insight and emotional connection. Out of touch, he failed to understand the situation and didn't factor the community into his decision-making. Consequently, his leadership was scrutinised because many saw him as insincere, seeking personal gain and political advantage while others suffered.

The approval ratings of each of the three leaders were measured immediately after the bushfires. To me, it is evident that the emotional and authentic approach by Andrews and Berejiklian won support and trust from both sides of politics, with 58 and 55 per cent respectively. The PM much less so with just 32 per cent approval (Lewis, 2020).

 Feeling

It's OK to feel. The 2019 Deloitte Human Capital Trends Survey highlighted the need for more human interaction and feeling at work as a way to increase productivity. The report explained that employee communication and engagement needs more than simple information transfer (telling). Leaders in this decade need to look beyond old ways, as human interaction now drives a better employee experience (Deloitte, 2019).

As indicated earlier, this is to be expected in our current workforce. Feeling and empathy are valued significantly by both employees and employers as ways to build better results. How we feel as leaders or employees impacts how we work, lead and interact with others. Once aware of our feelings and those of others, we can navigate and communicate better. The ultimate outcome of a better connection with employees is increased trust in you as a leader. Here are some ways you can use your feelings more at work.

It's OK to open up

Say how you feel about issues or situations at work. If you have concerns, then raising them will create a safe space for others to follow your example. Mutual feelings enhance collaboration and outcomes. Evidence has repeatedly shown that when leaders talk openly, they create a more trusting workspace. This sets the scene for others to do the same and allows employees to open up.

It's OK to show you care

We have been led to believe that having emotions or feelings at work is contrary to being efficient and productive. I think that is an outdated approach to leadership and work. Many studies and evidence now show the importance of emotion and mental health as a significant part of motivation and productivity.

We spend so much time at work that our health (and specifically mental health) is a key part of our success. The US Centre for Disease Control (CDC) says 'poor mental health and stress can negatively affect employee job performance and productivity, engagement with one's work, communication with co-workers, physical capability and daily functioning' (Nhaissi, 2019).

Checking in, asking about your employee's feelings (R U OK?) and mental health is the right thing to do. It shows you care and helps build connection and trust. Showing you are human with feelings too, creates a sense of belonging and connection with you as a leader. For those in any doubt, 'R U OK?' is a question we can ask any day, not just when prompted as part of an annual campaign.

It's OK to speak up

The ability to be yourself and speak your views is not a universal experience at work. Many organisations have cultures that limit, rather than permit, the open sharing of opinions. Team members who can challenge each other constructively or have divergent views are more creative, supportive of failure and can move beyond potential differences.

Behavioural scientist Amy Edmondson coined the term 'psychological safety'. It describes the 'belief that you won't be punished or humiliated for speaking up with ideas, questions, concerns or mistakes'. Her research showed that failing or making mistakes is part of how we learn. So if there is a fear of errors in the team, then we are likely limiting our learning. In the same way, if we are fearful of speaking up or offering views, then we limit ideas, information sharing and progress (Edmondson, 2018).

Having psychological safety in your team enables significantly better teamwork. Google researchers found that when team members feel safe to make mistakes and be vulnerable in front of each other, they can be more successful. If there is a fear of asking for or giving constructive feedback in teams or a hesitance around asking 'silly' questions, then managers need to improve psychological safety.

You can find more in this useful guide to boosting psychological safety in your team at https://rework.withgoogle.com/print/guides/5721312655835136/

It's OK to feel embarrassed

Leigh Thompson, Professor at Illinois's Northwestern University, wrote that telling an embarrassing story about ourselves improves psychological safety and can make some conversations or meetings more creative and productive. Participants in discussions or brainstorming sessions feel greater trust in their peers once they have all shared an awkward moment or been candid about a situation.

Thompson proposed a new rule for brainstorming sessions: Tell a self-deprecating story before you start. As uncomfortable as this may seem, especially among colleagues you would typically want to impress, the result will be a broader range of creative ideas (Thompson, 2017).

BPAY: Show that you care

'Pandemic transition has been easy because of our culture and set up. We have daily communications from the leadership team and all staff meetings regularly. We keep it real and upbeat, but at the same time, we are honest and human. For example, this morning, I sent two people a happy birthday message. These things make a difference'. John Banfield, CEO, BPAY

 **Listening**

I know from personal experience the impact of a lack of listening, as my wife often says I don't listen. (Yes, it's a complete irony given my passion for communication!) But as a result, I am more aware that while hearing is the subconscious act of registering noise in your brain, listening is something much more proactive as a response to that sound.

Oscar Trimboli, the author of *Deep Listening,* says: 'Impactful communication isn't just about how eloquently and persuasively you speak. It's how consciously, deliberately and skilfully you listen' (Trimboli, 2017).

Trimboli says that not listening at work can lead to confusion, conflict or chaos, creating silos, waste and impacts that detract from our results. When leaders fail to listen to employees, they miss opportunities to change or improve.

Focusing on listening is a major step toward powerful conversations. When leaders listen, they open up a treasure chest of ways to motivate, excite and unite their employees. We learn about our people's preferences and needs so we can meet our own needs and those of the organisation. Listening is one of the easiest but least used senses we all have that can help improve communication and leadership. But listening doesn't just happen. We need to be proactive about creating opportunities to listen if we are to really get under the skin of who our people are and what they need.

A case study

The sporting goods retailer, Decathlon, employs about 85,000 staff globally, with more than 120 stores. Online reviews by their employees describe their amazing work culture, and it's no surprise to find vitality and responsibility as their global values. Their Australian CEO, Olivier Robinet, has a 92 per cent approval rating by employees and 80 per cent of employees say they would recommend a friend to work there. Decathlon has more than 2,000 employee reviews on Glassdoor, and most of these are very positive.

Decathlon is an excellent example of a business that reformed and evolved to listen more and make employee participation a priority for leaders. They have a non-traditional approach to management, which refers to the level of involvement and listening undertaken by leaders. The happiness of his team is Robinet's first KPI, and the happiness of his customers is second.

Every month staff are surveyed, and those who are not completely happy to come to work every day, sit down with a self-appointed coach and other staff to work out their problems. 'It's our company – we are a human company, we are not a financial company,' says Robinet. 'Financial for us is very important, but it is just a consequence of what we do. If my team is happy, they will do a very good job. If you want to have this culture, it's not easy; you need to have good managers, good coaches, you need to listen a lot' (Mitchell, 2017).

Collective listening

Remember: you already have all the tools and abilities you need to be able to listen more effectively. Some focus and practise will improve your understanding of your landscape and get better results. When teams listen collectively, they learn and hear much more together. Group listening is like being in a herd of antelope on the savannah. They survive and thrive by using their collective sense of listening to avoid getting eaten by predators. In this way, listening collectively as a business can create benefits for your entire herd!

I recently interviewed Alex Goryachev, MD of Innovation at Cisco Systems. A multinational technology conglomerate based in Silicon Valley, they develop, make and sell IT networking hardware, software, telecommunications equipment and other high-technology services and products. Cisco has around 75,000 employees globally, and is known for an 'inclusive atmosphere of ongoing employee innovation'.

Alex helps foster creative ideas from employees and supports the organisation to turn them into new products and services. He sparks internal innovation by providing employees at all levels the chance to share their big ideas, many of which make their way into the company's innovation engine.

'A great example of an innovation coming from everyday employees is the PlayStation, which originated as an idea from a (then) junior-level Sony employee named Ken Kutaragi. Upper-level management dismissed his idea, but Kutaragi persisted, and today the Sony PlayStation is the best-selling gaming console of all time.

'To create innovative ideas, we need to empower every single employee to innovate. Innovation is not just about new products or top-line growth. We need leaders to redefine what innovation means. It's not only technology – it could also be processes, systems, business models – simply anything that brings value to the company. This way, everyone can contribute. Leaders listen, engage and get better ideas that produce a lasting impact. At Cisco, we are fortunate to have the sponsorship of our CEO and the support of all functions. We have developed this project with all key leaders to help make this a top priority.

'Often, employees know more about your products or services than the C-Suite or board members because they are the closest to customers and markets. Often the best thing that corporate leaders can do is to go and listen to the field and their customers. And let employees show them the way.'

Listening to the 'said'

The 'said' isn't just what comes up in conversations or meetings; it includes the results of surveys, data, complaints and feedback. We take action on this information by listening and routinely empowering employees to implement useful suggestions and try new ways of working.

The following examples will provide insights into your team from what is said. Remember, if you are ever unsure of what is being said, take the time to clarify your conclusion with those who said it.

- Employee Engagement Survey Results and individual comments: These are mandatory listening for every leader.
- Recognition: Notice who is getting recognition in your business. What motivated them to succeed?

- Exit Surveys: Find out why employees are leaving. Take action to improve.
- Complaints: Understand why they arose and address the root causes.
- Compliments: Understand what sparked them and create conditions for more.

Listening for the 'unsaid'

The 'unsaid' is less straightforward than the 'said', but can be more impactful to tap into once you understand your employees.

The unsaid are often behavioural indicators of engagement or trust that aren't measured in surveys. They can exist elsewhere in the organisation, within formal data sets including sick days, incidents, awards won or compliments. The unsaid are behavioural outcomes of low or high employee engagement. They don't necessarily show up in the annual engagement survey results, but they happen every day. The unsaid are key listening points we need to tune in to.

Unsaid behaviours can also manifest in team reactions or responses. They are part of the team's culture. People act in ways that demonstrate how they feel. Body language is the classic unsaid, e.g. an eye-roll. At work, the unsaid might appear as a request ignored by a team member or a surprise sick day. All provide data for good leaders to consider.

Seeing around corners

Listening helps leaders to learn the typography of their workforce or business. I learned more about this when talking with Simon Harris, Managing Director of Open Door Management and Founder of Nomad Spaces. His expertise is in luxury hospitality operations and people leadership. Simon says a key skill for leaders is the ability to see around corners. Leaders need to listen to anticipate what's ahead and be proactive. He believes leaders need to help others to do the same. Listening is an essential strategy here. Given his deep insight into motivating service cultures, I asked him what makes a great communicator.

'Great communication is about empathy, listening, understanding. In hospitality, if you want to know the employee sentiment or what is going on in the business or the hotel, you ask the room attendants. They know the business best. To learn about the pulse of the business, you have to connect with the coalface. It's the same in hospitality as other more corporate environments. Leaders need to make decisions based on facts, not their assumption of employees' needs.'

 # Thinking

Rational thoughts, reasoning and conversation have enabled humans to excel. Our ability to think of others and work as a team sets us apart from most other life-forms. In the same way, a leader who thinks and acts on behalf of their team can provide the information and environment it needs to excel.

> 'A lot of leaders are frightened to tell the truth because they are worried about what people will think. It goes back to being kind instead of nice. We are all adults at work. So if you skirt around something then drop a bomb, you will blindside employees and lose trust. We have to consider people and their situations.'
> – *Michael Schneider, MD, Bunnings*

Thinking on behalf of your team requires effort. Leaders who do so have invested time into using their super-powers to translate business objectives and plans into employee conversations. They do this having gained employee insights and connected with them. You can translate business needs into actions for the team by building a mental picture of their preferences and needs. This will enable you to answer critical questions and help the team to soar. Those who cannot think for their team or translate corporate-speak are most likely causing their team to sink.

Sinking, not thinking

Failing to consider team members in your decisions and actions reduces their trust in your leadership. If you cannot translate the corporate strategy into meaningful actions for them, they may well see you as redundant. Other outcomes might be reduced opportunities, limited resources, impacted budgets and demotivated team members. If you hear yourself think or say some of the following when making decisions or communicating, you might be sinking your team:

- I don't care how you feel about this, just get on with it.
- It's not that big a deal, can we just move on?
- The team is paid to do this work so it will have to suck it up.
- I really don't have time for these questions.
- It's a management decision, and we have to implement it, like it or not.
- I don't want a quicker way. I just want it sorted.
- I don't need to hear about your family drama.
- I'm not paid enough to deal with these people.
- I'm way too busy for a monthly team meeting.
- How many times do I need to explain this?

Thinking and soaring

Using insights and considering the team in your decisions and actions, boosts team support for decisions, gains momentum and builds trust. Leaders of soaring teams consistently think about their team's situation, response and needs. These leaders think on behalf of their team, accurately gauging what the team might do or say in given situations. This does not always come easily, but can be learned. Translating business plans into team and employee actions takes consideration and practise.

The easiest way to learn how to think on behalf of your team is to imagine how it might react in a given situation. Your knowledge of each team member's personality or mindset will help you to imagine how they might feel, react or respond.

Using your insights about your team to inform your decisions and actions will help you and your team to soar. Leaders who create this environment typically ask themselves key questions each time there is something that might impact their team.

Ten questions to help you consider your team in decisions:

- What does the team need to succeed?
- What is holding the team back?
- How would this impact or benefit my team?
- What can I do to support my team in this?
- How can I build enthusiasm for this in the team?
- What actions can we take as a team to support this goal?
- What questions might the team have?
- Have I set a clear direction on this?

- What questions are the team asking, and what is this telling me about their situation?
- How might the team be feeling given its current situation?

It's not all about you!

A few years ago, I led a major office relocation. It was the worst kept secret (they always are), and I was supporting the Executive team to engage the 1,500 employees in the move. It was a big ask as the new location was an hour away, in a less popular area.

One Senior Executive (not known for compassion or subtlety) suggested emailing everyone to announce the big news. He was sure the news would be welcomed and that any resistance would blow over in a few months. This was not the engagement strategy I had in mind.

It turned out that he would benefit from the relocation, as it was significantly closer to his family home. We had a long conversation about how great it would be to have a reduced commute. He talked about looking forward to having more time with his family, lower fuel costs and more time to do sport before or after work. All fair points.

I then asked how it might feel if those were taken away? How would he feel if his commute was increasing and time with family diminished? He quickly realised it wasn't all about him, and for this project to succeed, he had to consider the situation and emotions of others.

As leaders, we need to remember there is always another side to any scenario, and that some employees will need a deeper conversation to get behind our decisions. Information alone is not enough to gain emotional support from the workforce.

Giving

Learning the preferences of your team members will help you provide what they need to thrive. Giving them more of what they need enhances their sense of belonging, which is a key motivator for the 2020 workforce.

> ❝ As leaders we need to think of our audience and what is appropriate for them. We need to model behaviours and traits that we want others to adopt, not preach to them. This helps creates trust. Be generous. Acknowledge others and the contribution they make. Drive out fear so that others feel like they can contribute and be open and honest. You have to be quite selfless to influence and change others. You have to keep thinking about what a change means for them, what is relevant to them and how best to communicate. ❞
>
> *– Angela Tsoukatos, Executive Coach*

Being a *giving* leader takes time and effort. It doesn't always come naturally – especially to those who believe the team is there to serve them. In the past, leaders needed to be strong, deliver on goals, drive performance and generally get stuff done. However, the language and thinking around this has changed significantly in recent years – as has the way we motivate others.

Now more than ever, leaders appreciate that employees want to achieve a shared vision, not just serve their leader. Our role is to coach employees and enable them to be high performing. Our giving is an act that fuels the fire under our teams. When employees thrive, then our jobs become much more straightforward, and our results grow.

Give support

Being supportive was deemed the most important leadership behaviour in a 2019 McKinsey survey (Feser, et al., 2015). So, to get a better understanding of what employees need, try asking how best you can work together. These might help you start the conversation at one of your employee catch-ups:

- How do you best work in a team?
- Under what conditions do you create your best results?
- How would you prefer to receive feedback? In-person or in writing?
- How much is team interaction important to you?
- How would you like to be recognised for your work? Do you prefer verbal praise in front of others, or more privately?
- How much direction or context do you like before kicking off a project?

- Do you prefer to listen and come back with questions or ask them straight away? Or both?

Give them a voice

Creating a communication culture in your team gives everyone a voice, creating trust in you and the team. To do this, build habits that help you regularly listen to employees. Join in existing or start new conversations. Here are some ways that enable employees to speak while you are actively listening.

- Ask high performers why they stay with the organisation. Give them more of what makes them happy.
- Host a regular gathering with a group of employees (e.g. a team breakfast) to listen and connect.
- Have a regular event to listen to front-line leaders: these supervisors are your eyes and ears too!
- Make small-talk, be curious: you will be surprised who you meet or what you learn in the lift or the lobby of your building.
- Spend time where the real work conversations happen: at the canteen, coffee shop, water-cooler.
- Shadow an employee for the day: get on the tools!
- Follow the 80 per cent listening and 20 per cent speaking rule when leading your meetings.
- Hold a focused discussion about a priority: safety, customers, strategy, growth.
- Put your questions out on the internal social media platform: see what comes back

How do you learn to listen?

'Give it a go. Sit with the discomfort of not talking for a while and just listen. This can be hard for those not used to doing it, but it is very rewarding. It's uncomfortable at first. You don't have to say yes to everything you hear. Acknowledge what you hear. Stop thinking you need to know all the answers. Try to remember that it's OK just to have questions. Give it a go. The sun will come up tomorrow if it doesn't go as planned.' – Bronwyn Evans, CEO, Engineers Australia

But don't give them a vote

While employee opinions and input fuel our results, businesses still need direction and decision-making from leaders. That's our job. However, to drive impact and lead effectively, leaders need to create clarity. They must discount views or ideas that are not on strategy, and channel effort productively. We have to be able to explain why we make certain decisions – not just mandate them. The reasoning behind our decisions is a major driver of trust. In this way, when tackling issues of importance, the best leaders give employees a voice, but not a vote.

In an *HBR* article, Botelho, Powell, Kincaid and Wang wrote that these leaders listen and solicit views but do not default to consensus-driven decision-making. They quoted Christophe Weber, CEO of Takeda Pharmaceutical who makes a habit of having unstructured meetings with 20 to 30 of the company's high potentials to give them a voice before making key decisions. The goal of those meetings is to challenge him and present him with new perspectives, but he is careful not to create the illusion of democracy. He believes that consensus is good, but it's too slow, and sometimes you end up with the lowest common denominator (Lytkina Botelho, et al., 2017).

Be giving during crises

Fifteen years ago, I spent three years in London, planning communication for the UK national response to a potentially deadly pandemic. The focus was on national actions, global impacts and high stakes scenarios. We considered complexity and in-depth scenario planning that might gain community trust and keep the public calm. We were thinking at a high level on the big stuff, but we had no idea what a real pandemic, years later, would actually be like.

As leaders, we are often encouraged to focus on big picture challenges such as culture, strategy and outcomes. But during a crisis, it is smaller-scale actions that help us stick together and make the difference. Rather than providing strategic direction, a crisis requires a change in giving strategy to communicate things that provide our team with comfort, reality and structure so they can keep moving forward.

During crises, leaders who thrive communicate a much closer horizon. They meet the basic needs of their teams by communicating what is important right here and now. In the early 2000s, when planning the pandemic response, we didn't factor in the need for conversation, companionship or belonging. Yet these are exactly what will hold our teams, businesses and communities together. Here are some tips for switching your communication during a crisis to deal with unpredictability, chaos or isolation.

Replace fear with familiarity

If the situation is volatile or we are unable to predict we should:

- Connect regularly — schedule meetings, calls or Zoom sessions with employees who are working remotely.
- Create a simple purpose for your team in times of complexity.
- Make them feel safe with your continuity.

Beat chaos by creating structure

If the proverbial hits the fan and it's all going off:

- Be clear on what is tight and what is loose in the team.
- Set clear expectations about rules and roles while the team is dispersed or overwhelmed.
- Clarity and consistency are engaging for employees. Wishy-washy leadership without boundaries does nothing for anyone.

> **❝ Communication is your ticket to success, if you pay attention and learn to do it effectively. ❞**
> *– Theo Gold*

To gain control: empower others

If you feel events are beyond your control:

- Set up your team members so they are in control of their contribution. Ensure they have the tools they need.
- Enable the team to make decisions.
- Make every team member feel part of the solution or plan.

Build a community to counter isolation

If you are spread out or across different sites:

- Create belonging with opportunities to come together.
- Create conversations to connect the team.
- Be human and forgiving. We are all still learning, even during a crisis.

 # Tasting

There is no substitute for first-hand experience. My wife was bold enough to jump out of a plane and skydive. It is something I would love to do, and she has explained the feeling and experience countless times. But I won't ever understand until I have tasted the experience for myself.

Benjamin Franklin said, 'An investment in knowledge always pays the best interest.' That is why companies spend more than US$47 billion on market research each year (Palacio, 2019). It enables them to connect and build relationships with their customers. If businesses did not make products or services that customers valued or desired, then they would fail. In the same way, leaders need to understand employees to ensure their leadership style hits the mark.

Leaders who build a mental picture of each of their team members, understand employee preferences and use these for their success. Think about personality types in your team and how best to use these. When allocating work, would you give numbers and budgets to manage to the creative big picture thinkers who aren't good with details? Or would you ask the detail-focused numbers geek to crunch the numbers for you? I know who I would prefer for that task. Understanding the interests and styles of your team helps you have more powerful conversations.

I agree with Benjamin Franklin — investing time in learning helps us engage more easily. Time with your team is a leader's market research. The insights gained help maximise your impact, hit the mark in your communication and inspire and unite the team in your quest.

Here are real-life examples of how some leaders have tasted the world of employees:

- Shadow an employee for the day: See things first-hand.
- Spend time on the tools — at the call centre or on the truck with the operators.
- Spend the day at another site or workplace: Each worksite will have a sub-culture of the whole organisation.

- Attend the corporate induction: These usually reveal a lot about the business (for better or worse!).

- Schedule a regular site visit: Theme it with a focus, e.g. on safety, customers or innovation.

- Take part in regular campaigns/activities, e.g. awareness days and fundraising events.

- Take the time to connect with employee protagonists, in person and on social media; they usually have the lowdown.

- Hold regular town hall meetings and ensure they align with employee needs and your strategy.

- Invite them in: Hold a listening event and ask the questions you want insights on.

Remember: Seeing things first-hand helps create emotional intelligence.

Speaking

Language, conversation and voice make us human. In a world overtaken by electronic and digital communication, I believe speaking is much less used but significantly more important for leaders. Speaking is one way to humanise ourselves and others. Relying on email and text messages to communicate will never succeed because employees won't fully trust us.

Charles Dickens was right when he wrote: 'Electric communication will never be a substitute for the face of someone who, with their soul, encourages another person to be brave and true.'

That is why we need to use our speaking super-power wisely: it enables us to encourage others to strive, achieve and deliver. A leader's words and voice create change, innovation and results. Consider these approaches to ensure you harness your speaking super-power to yield the required impact and results.

Put face-to-face first

Putting face-to-face communication at the top of your list of communication channels will positively influence your results. First-hand engagement with leaders that includes eye contact shows you take the conversation seriously. Taking the time to speak in this way will increase your authenticity, reinforce your personal brand and grow trust. All of which will boost your results.

DIY

Don't rely on others to deliver messages on your behalf. Do it yourself, and deliver your own message, irrespective of the content. As we discussed in Chapter Five, outsourcing your communication reduces its impacts, erodes trust and misses the point. FYI, outsourcing includes passing the buck to your deputy or avoiding giving bad news.

Make eye contact

When having a conversation, the golden rule for many in the Western world is to look into the eyes of the person you are talking to. They are right there in front of you, so this really shouldn't be hard.

Smile

It's accepted that smiling makes people trust you more and helps improve your personal productivity (Forbes, 2010). You will be surprised how much this simple gesture improves perceptions of you too, and that means more trust in you as leader.

Ask

I hope that by this stage, I don't need to re-state the importance of asking over telling. Asking is part of leading.

> ❝ I often witness, contrary to popular belief, that middle managers are the most innovative part of organisations. My advice to corporate leaders is to ask them and all employees more questions. It's OK to say 'I don't know. What do you think? ❞
> — *Alex Goryachev, MD of Innovation, Cisco*

I was interested to learn insights from the pandemic experience from the Bunnings perspective. MD, Michael Schneider, explained: 'The beauty of the internal social media platform enabled us to connect directly with our team and them with us. It's really important that that happens. You learn from these kind of platforms where the gaps really are in communication and leadership.

'For example, some of the recent actions we took came from leaders listening to the fear or confusion of team members on the front line about safety.

'If you don't have the front-line connection, then you are at risk of believing middle managers telling you that everyone is happy and fine and doing a great job.

'Some employees were scared senseless during the Covid-19 crisis. They were dealing with lots of people who might have been infected. The voices from the front line have helped us realise some good learnings when it comes to customer and team safety in that respect.'

REFLECT

Five Takeaways:

- Learn about your team
- Build a connection
- Talk less
- Listen more
- Gain trust.

Three Questions:

- How will you use your super-powers to improve understanding of your employees?
- What habits are you going to build that will help you listen and connect more?
- How are you using your understanding of the team when you communicate?

One Quote:

❝ You can be the most brilliant innovator, problem-solver or strategic thinker, but if you can't inspire and motivate, build relationships or communicate powerfully, those talents will get you nowhere. ❞

– Daniel Goleman

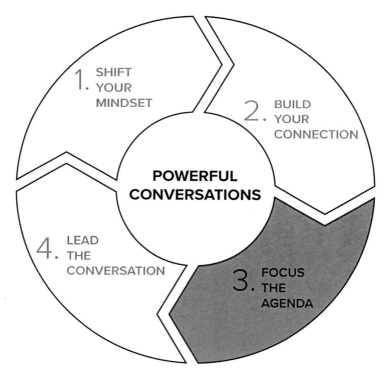

Figure 10: Focus the agenda

8

Focus the Agenda

The foolproof way to ensure your leadership is relevant and purposeful is by prioritising and focusing on the right conversations. Aligning what we do and say to the business strategy and the needs of the team sets clear parameters for powerful conversations.

This chapter highlights a framework on which to base our interactions with employees. We explore key employee questions, how you can anchor conversations and employees consistently to the business strategy and how your clarity counts when setting the direction.

We are all so preoccupied at work. It seems few people have spare time or capacity to take on more. There is so much change happening and who knows that lies ahead if 2020 is anything to go by! As leaders and employees, we are not just time-poor but increasingly attention-poor. Our ability to stay focused on a piece of communication or a discussion has become compromised by infinite connections and information on phones, social media and elsewhere. All of these have led me to believe that everything we say and do as leaders should have a crystal clear purpose.

This chapter explores how those leaders who make the most impact consistently link their communication to the priorities of the team. Those who don't, habitually risk losing attention or not meeting goals.

Call them to action

> *In an information-rich world...a wealth of information creates a poverty of attention.*
> – Herbert A. Simon (Nobel Prize winner)

You don't have to be a Nobel Prize winner to work out that most people don't have time for pointless conversations. So, when leaders communicate, it needs to be purposeful, for everyone. Each of our communications or conversations should have an action or outcome aligned to the bigger picture or a plan. Sounds simple, but you would be surprised by the amount of 'passive' communication that has no alignment to a business goal. During my two decades of working in corporate Europe and Australia, I have received some very finely crafted corporate emails and had multiple conversations with important, time-poor people that fail to say anything or encourage action on a goal. This communication is a massive waste of energy, time and opportunity.

Some examples of formal communication that lack purpose might include:

- Meetings with no subject or agenda or that just seem to go on forever
- Emails that don't get to the point or give readers action or insight
- Conversations that fail to achieve anything because they have no goal or limit
- General indecision.

Decision and direction are the currency of time-poor leaders. So, the following checklist should help ensure your conversation or email gets to the point and creates action.

Purpose Checklist

- What do I want to achieve?
- Why am I doing this?
- What do I want the attendees or recipients to do?
- Which goal does this link to and how?
- Does the conversation include a call to action?
- Have I agreed the follow-up or next steps?
- Am I informed enough to have this conversation now?
- Do I need more information before I communicate this?

Engaging a workforce of 1.4 million employees

I have seen first-hand that, with focus and effort, the right conversations can transform cultures and save thousands of lives.

In London (years ago) I worked on a behaviour and cultural transformation across every English hospital. Our vision was to halve the number of infections caused by poor clinical behaviour (such as doctors not washing their hands).

I worked for an inspirational leader, Janice. Her mission was for all English hospitals to raise safety and care standards by ensuring every employee practised safely. It was a major challenge in an organisation of over 1.4 million healthcare employees, treating one million patients every day.

I will never forget Janice's mantra. Her absolute commitment was to getting leaders and clinicians to 'focus effort and action at infection hot-spots' to get the biggest bang for their buck. In other words, we wanted employees to ensure they did the high-risk and high-impact things that would move further and faster towards our vision.

We provided consistent advice to hospitals on how to target hot-spots and encourage their teams to focus. Over three years and with significant effort and action, it worked! We halved the number of infections in hospitals, improved clinical care and saved thousands of lives. It was a world-first that improved the public perception of English hospitals.

We succeeded in changing the culture and behaviour of one of the world's largest workforces. Focused leadership conversations were at the heart of this transformation, as leaders reinforced the role and contribution of employees to our target. Leaders engaged every member of the hospital team from the Board to the ward. Every team member knew their role and made their contribution to saving lives.

Clarity counts

We have all been in situations where we were unsure of which direction to go. Limited or poor information from a colleague or leader can set us off in the wrong direction or paralyse us for fear of doing the wrong thing. Clarity helps employees access the facts and get direction. Without it, teams can lose productivity and relevance. Setting clear direction and expectations can make a significant difference to outcomes, results and energy in a team.

Bring me a dog!

Earlier this year, I was coaching a CEO from a financial marketing business, who was frustrated by the level of questions, rework and duplication in his team. He said it was easier for him to do things himself rather than 'explain things five times'. This got me wondering about his level of clarity and how he communicated with his teams. As we talked, it became clear that his requests to others were vague. No wonder he wasn't getting what he needed.

I delved deeper into his style of leadership and discovered he was unspecific about timelines and used general rather than specific terms in his conversations. He frequently had to 'send team members away to rethink stuff'.

So, I did what any decent coach would do. I asked him to go and 'bring me a dog'.

Intrigued, he suggested some breeds I might want.

'Pug?

Spaniel?

Staffy?

Poodle?' He guessed.

'No.... Keep trying,' I replied, shaking my head.

He eventually got frustrated and gave up. He couldn't guess which dog to bring me because I had been intentionally unspecific. I had purposely made it hard for him to succeed by being vague. He became disengaged because I was clear on what I didn't want, not what I did.

Then we started over, and I asked him again to bring me a dog. Only this time, I was clear about my needs: medium in size, white, black spots and a breed that rhymes with damnation.

He immediately responded to the request with a big smile: 'Dalmatian!'

We reflected on the two conversations. The impact of my first request was deflating, frustrating and made it almost impossible for him to succeed. He began thinking about how his employees must have felt when dealing with his vagueness.

The second request was crystal clear, and the response was efficient and engaging. It respected his time and mine because it had clarity.

My client later reflected on his own 'bring me a dog' style conversations, realising how this was impacting his team and himself. His style created unnecessary obstacles and didn't empower his team to deliver solutions.

I have thought about clarity a lot over the years and how sometimes leaders are caught up in a 'curse of knowledge'. This can create the presumption that others know what we are talking about or understand us because we know what we mean. But perhaps they don't and need more context or detail.

Check your clarity

When it comes to creating clarity for your team, just how explicit are you? Are you only clear with yourself? Cursed with your own knowledge? Or does everyone on the team understand? The Be Clear model below is a simple way to check your clarity.

❮ Clarity affords focus. ❯

– Thomas Leonard

BE CLEAR

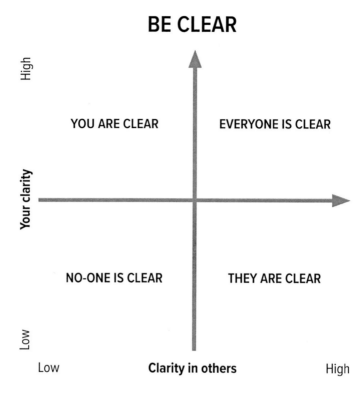

Figure 11: Be Clear model

You are clear

You might be clear with yourself, but perhaps others are lost or don't get it. Check with your team or audience to ensure you are on the same page.

They are clear

Everyone else might be clear, but you are lost. Find out whether what you think aligns with what the team thinks.

No-one is clear

Sometimes everyone can be on different pages. The best way forward is to have a conversation and decide on a way forward. Move to a place where everyone understands and agrees.

Everyone is clear

Clarity is where we want to land — the place where your perception or understanding is the same as your team's. By consistently checking in on direction and expectations, you can maintain clarity — a productive and creative space where you can move forward together and achieve more.

What actions will move you towards the top right quadrant? This is where powerful conversations happen. Think about how you can help team members to be clear. Are you empowering them with the right amount of information? Are you specific without being constricting in your requests? Too much or too little information can be restrictive and disengaging. Is your team culture open enough for members to ask clarifying questions? Or are you asking them to bring you dogs?

> ❛ Without focusing and getting to clarity
> you cannot lead. You cannot motivate. You
> cannot plan. You cannot communicate. ❜
> – *Bobbi Biehl*

SWITCH

Provide translation

There is nothing more frustrating for employees than corporate jargon, business speak or language they can't understand. It feels exclusive or overly complicated. Not only that – trying to work out someone else's poor communication wastes time and destroys energy and engagement. Complex language forces us to spend unnecessary time working out what is needed. It delays action and turns us off, not switches us on.

Simple, plain words that get to the point keep us focused and ensure clarity for the recipient.

Gabrielle Dolan is an educator, author and the founder of Jargon Free Fridays. She is on a mission to change the way businesses communicate. Gabrielle wants to move away from the default of corporate jargon that disconnects and isolates people, to stories and language that connect and engage (Dolan, n.d.).

This is the ultimate purpose of leader communication. We have a responsibility to translate business strategy and corporate narratives into meaningful, simple, engaging conversations and actions for employees. Translation is a vital skill for leaders now and in the future.

Leaders who create clarity have built their skill of translation. They can break down and explain complex messages and leadership decisions so that employees can connect with them. These leaders invest time understanding their business plan and carve it into meaningful actions and projects for their team. Then they set direction and clarity

154

that supports the team to deliver results, aligned to the vision. In this way, everything the team focuses on is aligned to a business outcome. It is a straightforward way to help leaders keep their teams focused on business priorities, ensuring relevance internally and externally.

In this sense, translation creates clarity and alignment between employees, the team and the organisation. Many leaders ask 'What do I need to translate?' and 'How much detail do employees need?' To help ensure leaders are building clarity in their team, I have designed four critical questions. These help leaders focus on what employees need to thrive and help employees understand where they fit in and what they need to do to succeed.

> ❝ I always did something I was a little not ready to do. I think that's how you grow. When there's that moment of 'Wow, I'm not really sure I can do this,' and you push through those moments, that's when you have a breakthrough. ❞
>
> *— Marissa Mayer*

Clarity questions for leaders

Use these four questions to understand the needs of employees. Answering them regularly in your employee conversations will ensure your team members are clear on the direction of the organisation, how they fit in, their performance criteria and future.

- What is our vision?
- What is my role?
- How will I be measured?
- What does my future entail?

REFLECT

Five Takeaways:

- Focus on a plan or an outcome
- Anchor communication to business goals
- Translate the strategy
- Be clear
- Reinforce direction.

Three Questions:

- Have you answered the critical questions for every member of your team?
- Have you asked your leader your critical questions?
- Are you crystal clear in your communication?

One Quote:

> ❝ A lack of clarity could put the brakes on any journey to success. ❞
>
> – *Steve Maraboli*

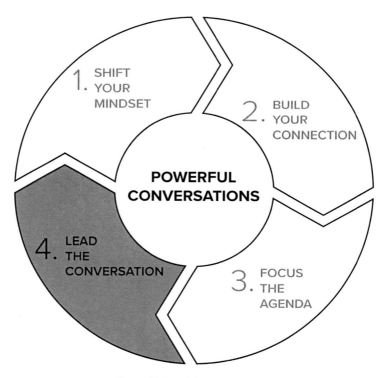

Figure 12: Lead the conversation

9

Lead the Conversation

The final stage of powerful conversations is where we activate our learning and thinking from the earlier sections of this book. It takes time to establish and needs a bit of practise or experimentation, using our growth mindset!

Leading a trusting and powerful conversation won't just happen overnight. With more frequent action, you will move to a place of trust and high engagement with significantly better results. To achieve this, you will need to focus on embedding trust in your communication and be committed to building a system that makes conversations effortless.

Build trust in how you lead

Trust is rocket fuel.

It is the number one currency for high employee engagement. With trust, we can achieve much more and go further faster. In this sense, building trust is like putting rocket fuel in our tank. It is a catalyst that enhances performance and helps us achieve more.

The following triangle reminds us of the three key aspects that build trust for leaders. When we stop telling and consistently demonstrate these elements, we lock in trust as *how* we lead because it is part of regular interactions with employees. When trust-building is our daily routine, the results can be breathtaking.

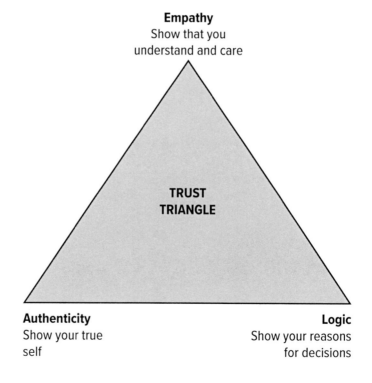

Figure 13: Trust triangle

Trust Builder	Asking...	Saying....
Empathy: How? Show that you understand and that you care by using your super-powers and insights	How are you? What do you need from me? How did the meeting go?	I understand how you feel... I feel the same.... I am happy for you...
Authenticity: How? Show your true self by admitting mistakes, asking for help, being open and inclusive	What could I improve on? What should I do more of? What should I do less of?	I am sorry... I don't know... I didn't realise...
Logic: How? Show reasons for your decisions while building clarity, alignment and translating business goals.	Does this make sense? Can you see why we are focusing on this? Explain how your idea links to our goal?	We are doing this because... My reasoning was... The data tells me...

Figure 14: Trust building questions

Leading the conversation in a way that locks in trust requires a focus on three aspects: Understanding conversations that engage, building a conversation infrastructure and making conversations habitual and systematic.

> ❝ When the trust account is high, communication
> is easy, instant, and effective. ❞
>
> *– Stephen R. Covey*

Understanding conversations that engage

There are four types of conversation that build trust and engage employees. Each anchors team discussion and action to the business strategy and the ability to get stuff done. They include:

- WHY conversations: align to the big picture vision, purpose or team plan
- WHAT conversations: focus our work on achieving goals
- WHO conversations: identifying roles to deliver results
- HOW conversations: create ideas and new ways

WHY conversations

The goal for a WHY conversation is to reinforce our purpose with logical explanations.

Effective WHY conversations are only possible when leaders understand their business strategy and vision. Logic anchors acceptance of our decisions. Employees don't always have to agree with the decisions, but explaining the reasons behind them helps to gain trust and create action.

A WHY conversation can explain the rationale for a decision or a business development: for example, leaders might get asked why the business acquired a new company or sold a part of the existing company? This WHY conversation might start something like this:

'Today we announced that we have sold the transportation part of our company. I wanted to explain why this has taken place [ESTABLISH CLARITY].

Our business vision is to achieve market leader status in the engineering sector. While transport was a successful part of the business, it no longer aligns to the new business vision. [WHY]

Therefore, we have sold the transportation business so we can concentrate more on one goal and one segment. The revenue from this sale will enable greater investment and focus on engineering without distraction from other projects. Focusing on less will help us move forward in the projects we have prioritised [LOGIC]

Does that make sense? [DISCUSSION]

What else would you like to know or ask? [INVOLVE]

I realise this is a sad day as we have said farewell to some long-standing colleagues. I feel sad too that we won't get to work with them from now on, but we have had some fun times working together. [EMPATHY]

I have known many of the transport team for more than ten years. I worked in that team as a fresh-faced graduate and have some good and bad memories!! [AUTHENTICITY].

As a team, we need to ensure our day-to-day work and decisions support the overall business vision.

That is our ultimate goal and the reason our team exists [TRANSLATION].

WHAT conversations

WHAT conversations set or reinforce a direction. These conversations support decision-making or prioritisation of certain actions over others. Typically, the WHAT conversation relates to actions or decisions we are going to take to achieve an outcome or purpose. They are vital for direction-setting.

For example, a leader might include clarifying the direction and approach for a relocation. A leader might host this conversation at a team meeting in this way.

Leader: I wanted to have a discussion about the office relocation. What are you concerned about, and what does everyone need to know to support this move?

Employee: Are we refitting the new office before we move in?

Leader: I am glad you asked that. I was wondering about that too because I love my stand-up desk and wanted to take it with me. [EMPATHY]

I was also concerned that we might need to hot-desk in the new building [AUTHENTICITY]. Did anyone else have any similar concerns?

[DISCUSSION]

Leader: Well, this move is part of our plan to reduce property costs. The move is going to enable many of us to work nearer home and with better technology [LOGIC]. One of the ways we can afford to do that is by using the existing furniture, not spending on new. So, we will be moving the furniture, not buying new.

A refit would cost more and would not allow us all to have better technology or enjoy remote working [LOGIC].

WHO conversations

The purpose of a WHO conversation is clarity on the role and contribution of employees. For example, an employee might ask 'What is my role in delivering the business vision?' Or during a team might ask for clarity on their contribution to a project.

To build employee clarity, I use this translation tool, which is a simple way to translate high-level business visions or goals into team and employee deliverables. It helps employees see where they fit in the bigger picture and supports clarity and alignment in conversations.

Remember that clarity on role and contribution to the team and business are significant enhancers of engagement and performance.

Translation tool

This helps employees see where they fit in the business.

Business vision	Insert business vision here		
Team goals	Insert team goal A	Insert team goal B	Insert team goal C
Individual employee goals	Insert projects or actions needed by employee, with timeline	Insert projects or actions needed by employee, with timeline	Insert projects or actions needed by employee, with timeline
Employee target	Insert quantifiable measure, with date	Insert quantifiable measure, with date	Insert quantifiable measure, with date

Figure 15: Translation tool template

Here is a real example used by one of my clients to explain their team and employee roles in delivering World Class Airline Operations.

Business vision	World Class Airline Operations		
Team goals	Put safety first	Improve customer services	Continuous improvement
Employee goals	Go home safe each day	Develop and implement an employee app that improves data capture by end of FY.	Improve maintenance times and reduce costs
Employee target	Zero incidents 100% PPE 100% training Proactive safety intervention.	App built by Sept, tested by Nov, implemented by Dec	10% improvement in time and 20% reduced costs this FY

Figure 16: Translation tool example

Clarifying team or project roles

When guiding the WHO conversation across a project team, I use **RACI** – an acronym for **Responsible, Accountable, Consulted, Informed**. Allocating individual employees or teams across the business to these categories helps manage the WHO conversation and builds clarity on who does what. This can be done as an exercise involving your team or a project team that needs clarity on roles.

Responsible: Those employees required to coordinate the day-to-day delivery of a project or outcome, e.g. the project manager or coordinator. They develop, build, plan and achieve.

Accountable: Those who have ultimate ownership of the project or outcome. They approve, decide, sponsor and endorse.

Consulted: Those asked to input or give opinions on how the project gets delivered. They support, influence and advise.

Informed: Those who are kept updated and have no direct influence over the project.

This format can also be used to build the WHO conversation with external stakeholders.

HOW conversations

The goal of a HOW conversation is to create ideas, then a consensus on HOW an employee or a team might move forward.

In Chapter Seven, we looked at how leaders can let go of lower-level work and empower employees to decide and create for themselves. The HOW conversation is where leaders learn to let go and facilitate the conversation instead of telling.

The HOW conversation is about providing focus and parameters for employees to find suitable solutions, rather than solving a problem ourselves.

Consider the following scenarios that demonstrate different outcomes when the leader comes up with a solution versus the team generating an idea.

The *leader*-generated idea sounds easier for the leader but costs more to implement as it depends on the leader being right.

The *team*-generated idea is also easily developed but is much more sustainable, productive and effective for the business and the leader. It's a win-win solution.

> If you want to improve the organization,
> you have to improve yourself and the
> organization gets pulled up with you.
> *– Indra Nooyi*

	When the leader solves the problem	When the team solves the problem
Proximity to the problem	Far removed	Closer to it
Ownership by the team	Low. The leader has to drive support.	High. Team naturally supports their idea.
Number of ideas generated	One or several as the ideas are limited to one brain.	Multiple as many views and brains create more ideas and thinking.
Stickiness and implementation	Needs constant effort by the leader to involve the team	The team makes it stick with ease. Owns it.
Cost to the business	High demand on leader and employee time.	Low demand on employee time.
Leader time and effort	High	Low
Team engagement	Low	High
Trust building	Poor or could erode trust	High, will build trust

Figure 17: Leader or team-generated solutions

In the HOW conversation, the leader switches from problem-solver to facilitator of solutions. Instead of coming up with the ideas themselves, this conversation enables leaders to create the conditions for others to do so. This could be in the form of a brainstorm, facilitated discussion or listing activity to identify options for a solution. Once the options or scenarios are listed, the leader's role is to help the team evaluate them and allocate responsibilities.

I recently had a conversation with Ted Stuckey, who was then Managing Director of QBE Ventures, a business that invests in early-stage technology companies. Ted reinforced the importance of HOW conversations that are leader led.

'Involvement and conversation are a panacea when it comes to innovation and change.' Ted described the importance of leaders creating HOW conversations across businesses, rather than relying on their own ideas: 'Organisations and leaders need to find ways to create conditions and environments where we can have crazy ideas and do so easily. This needs leadership by example. Part of Ted's role was to 'create these environments and encourage executives to create their own fertile settings. This is where the biggest impact and potential for ideas and change will be'.

A guide to hosting HOW conversations

- Identify the problem your team needs to solve
- Invite participants to a discussion
- Explain the problem, impacts, and why it's important this gets fixed
- Set boundaries for solutions, e.g. timeframes, budget and non-negotiables such as safety
- Encourage ideas from employees by a listing or brainstorming activity
- Provoke ideas by asking 'What about X or Y' solutions?

- Finalise the shared list of ideas
- Prioritise ideas together based on cost, ease of implementation of return on effort
- Decide HOW you will move forward
- Finally, empower employees to implement their idea.

Why should they care?

Before starting any conversation, consider who needs to be involved and what's in it for them. You should consider their needs as well as yours in deciding whether the conversation will be a good use of everyone's time. Here is a simple template to help you determine who should be included in your conversations.

Conversation: <Insert name of conversation here>

Purpose:

Desired outcome:

Name of invitee:	Reason for inclusion?
<Insert name>	<Insert reason for inclusion >

Figure 18: Template for deciding conversation participants

Building your conversation infrastructure

Just as roads and tunnels move humans around a city, your conversation infrastructure moves information, data and engagement around the business. It includes the formal and informal communication channels and systems you need to lead.

Anchor to priorities

Aligning team conversations with the existing business rhythm enables you to lead your own version. Most organisations have a planning or operating rhythm to hang these conversations off, and almost every business has a vision, purpose and values to which leaders can align team performance and behaviour conversations.

Aligning with agenda setters and milestones ensures you are having timely, relevant and purposeful conversations that engage employees with the priorities. Here are some examples on which to focus team discussions:

Agenda setters

- Vision
- Brand
- Corporate values
- Financial results.

Milestones

- Annual planning cycle
- Quarterly reporting
- Performance review cycle
- Annual awards
- Executive meetings.

Establish the right channels for your conversations

It is essential to build a set of channels that will host your conversations. These set the rhythm and create a natural system from which to lead, involve and enable progress.

The backbone of any leader's communication channels should include these three powerful platforms:

- Annual team planning session: aligned to the business plan
- Monthly team meeting: team-wide discussion
- Regular employee catch-ups: one-on-one discussions.

Let's explore the benefits of each channel and how you can use them to build trust and impact.

Channel: Annual team planning session

Benefit: A dedicated session to plan and align with the business strategy for the year ahead. This is a vital tool for the leader and the team as it enables you to build your plan, agree on team scope, build resources and agree to outcomes. It is also a good opportunity to discuss what might, or might not, be working well in the team.

The role of the leader: Facilitate a discussion, set direction and translate the business strategy into team goals.

Key skills for leaders: Direction-setting, translating and facilitating the team conversation with a clear purpose.

Channel: Monthly team meeting

Benefit: Protected time for team discussion and connection, focused on the team deliverables and outcomes. The meeting should be a safe space where team members feel they can raise ideas or roadblocks and share learning or suggestions.

The role of the leader: Clarify and reinforce the team's direction and enable action across the team.

Key skills for leaders: Listening, facilitating discussion and enabling employees to make decisions and take action.

Channel: Employee catch-ups

Benefit: Individual face-to-face time for you and your employees. The perfect way to ensure you are building trust. Ideal for listening and supporting each other and learning what the employee needs to be successful. These should be safe, closed-door meetings where either party can raise issues, recognition, problems or requests.

The role of the leader: Check alignment while reinforcing role and contribution of employees.

Key skills for leaders: Listening and translating to ensure alignment with values, goals and projects.

> ❝ We are stronger when we listen, and
> smarter when we share. ❞
>
> — *Rania Al-Abdullah*

Making trusting conversations habitual and systematic

Making trusting conversations effortless requires us to build a framework that ensures they happen as part of business as usual. The Three Rs — Rhythm, Reason and Results — are a simple way for leaders to build the framework and make conversations systematic.

Let's consider how each of these can help you build a system that factors trust in the way you lead and connect with your team.

Rhythm

When we build a communication rhythm, we create a consistent pace of conversations that energise and inform employees. Just like a song, the rhythm sets the pace and melody for the team. Remember in Chapter Eight, when you read that managers who consistently meet with their team are around three (yes, three!) times more likely to have engaged employees.

Run a monthly roundtable

'I run a CEO roundtable every month with 16 employees. No agenda. Ask anything you like. It's one hour long and the time just flies by. We have a great discussion about what is on people's minds. Some of the younger employees are so energetic, so thoughtful about the services they are providing for our clients. I am amazed at their levels of confidence too. It's normal for CEOs to meet employees at every level of an organisation these days.' – John Banfield CEO, BPAY

Reason

We have already discussed the importance of purpose and clarity. So remember to keep asking yourself, 'Why am I having this conversation, sending this email or giving this presentation?'. Each communication channel should have a reason or purpose that supports the team to achieve its vision. That reason helps you decide which channel to use for any given conversation. It also helps your audience understand what is being asked or needed of them.

Results

Just as each channel has a reason, they should also have a result in mind. Having an outcome for each conversation and channel ensures a better purpose, clear alignment to goals and greater clarity for all.

The following table is a real-life example of a leader from one of my clients using the Three Rs to lead the conversation with her team. She is an Operations Manager leading a team of front-line employees in a Sydney transportation business.

Rhythm	Reason	Results
Daily toolbox talk	Awareness (e.g., safety)	Delivery
Monthly employee catch-up	Reinforce priorities	Alignment
Monthly team meeting	Set direction	Clarity
Annual team away day	Strategy development	Direction

Figure 19: Rhythm, reason and results

Rituals and habits

There is no such thing as the perfect leader. But have you noticed that some leaders appear to have everything sorted, deliver on time and keep all their plates spinning at once? It seems effortless for these people. That's because they have built a formal rhythm and an informal support system that enables conversations to happen and stuff to get done.

❝ Goals are good for setting a direction, but systems are best for making progress. ❞
— James Clear

I created an informal support system to complement my rhythm by building in personal and team rituals. These helped me establish norms and behaviours for myself and my team that helped us succeed. We were able to communicate and work more effectively together and individually.

Rituals and habits are repeated processes that are familiar and done with comfort and ease. These approaches helped me embed communication into HOW I led, ensuring that employee conversations were part of my daily routine.

Let go

Have you ever been on a roller coaster and let go? I have. It doesn't feel right to lift your arms in the air at high speed or height, but letting go heightens the impact of the ride. In the same way, letting go of problems and involving others creates more solutions and ideas – some of which might also take your breath away!

Making a habit of letting go and routinely having more HOW conversations doesn't absolve you of the problem; instead, it increases ownership of the solution. It happens when you ask the team for help and seek input beyond your own thinking. It's a guaranteed way to stop feeling the need to solve all the team's problems yourself.

Letting go allows you to create the environment for more ideas, innovation and greater employee ownership in your team. Each of the communication channels in your rhythm is an opportunity to let go and create more engagement as the norm.

I need to solve all the problems in my team

I hear this often from leaders who are caught up in compliance or setting narrow boundaries for change. They feel they have to sort out all the problems in the team themselves. In reality, employees are better informed to solve problems, as they are closer to the causes and impacts. Often leaders make the mistake of not involving others and deprive them of the chance to contribute and own the outcome. In this way, leaders block engagement by not sharing the load. These behaviours are reflected in persistent feedback from employees who want to be more involved.

> **❛ Good communication is as stimulating as black coffee, and just as hard to sleep after. ❜**
> *– Anne Morrow Lindbergh*

Move from 'me' to 'we'

I recently worked with a highly stressed GM of Safety and Environment, who simply had to let go. She was frustrated by errors and issues arising from poor performance and unsafe practices in her team. She was holding on to all of the team's problems when her role was to ensure they were solved – not to solve them herself.

After our coaching discussion, it was obvious that her focus was on enforcing the rules, meeting compliance targets and coming up with solutions for others to implement. Her results reflected a compliance culture in her team. The team focused on presenting problems for her to solve because that was the norm she created.

After some feedback, the leader tried letting go. She focused on engaging her team in solving the problems, rather than handing them her own solutions and ideas. The result was greater team involvement that led to a stronger sense of ownership and creativity. Collective thinking and collaboration brought significantly better outcomes. Her communication shifted the focus of the team, so they came up with the ideas and implemented them.

> ❝ Communication can unleash talent
> and mean the difference between a
> culture of breathtaking innovation and
> a culture of eroding stagnation. ❞
> – *Alex Goryachev, MD of Innovation, Cisco*

Prioritising problems for the team to solve (and not enforcing your ideas) will free up time so you can focus on your work, rather than doing the work of your team.

Start? Stop? Keep?

Feedback helps us grow and learn, so, I regularly used to ask my peers and team to help me improve. But often asking for feedback can be awkward or take too much time. I started to use the Stop, Start, Keep framework and have found this removes any awkwardness.

At regular catch-ups (individually or in discussion at the monthly team meetings), I would ask my team what we could Stop, Start and Keep doing. This framework made it easier for us to give feedback in a simple, safe way without having to overthink. It created a consistent focus on improving and prioritising, which became part of my team culture.

The questions became a team ritual that removed pressure from the feedback conversations.

Try asking your team to come to the next catch-up or meeting with these in mind. It is an excellent tool for reviewing progress over the previous quarter or year, enabling you to prioritise certain activities and let others go.

Perhaps you can ask your team to help you improve how you communicate using this framework. Some safe and easy questions to use to help build this as a ritual might be:

- When it comes to communication, what should I Start, Stop or Keep doing?
- When it comes to team communication, what should we Start, Stop or Keep doing?
- What should we Start, Stop or Keep doing to improve collaboration in the team?

WDYT?

Often when we come up against problems, we ask others for help. It is a natural reaction to learn from others. When leading in certain business cultures, I found myself presented with lots of problems that were not mine, but the responsibility of the team to solve. My role was to ensure they got fixed, not to fix them personally.

These helped me learn that problems are an opportunity to be embraced as engagement moments in the team.

Instead of solving them myself, I would ask the employees, 'What do you think?' (or WDYT?) This empowered them to take ownership of the problem and implementation of their solution. It reduced my time spent on their problems and allowed me to set a direction on a solution.

When employees asked me to solve their problem, I used some of these questions to enlist their input and ownership:

- What do you think?
- Have you thought about a possible solution? What is it?
- How would you solve this problem if I wasn't here?
- Do you think this is something the team can discuss as a group?
- Have a deeper think about how you might solve this issue more sustainably.
- Can you come up with some options?
- What else?

> **He who does not trust enough,**
> **will not be trusted.**
>
> *– Lao Tzu*

Step back

Problems rarely happen in isolation in organisations. Asking yourself who needs to know and why they should be involved, helps to build a solution that sticks.

Often we are not the best person to solve a problem, but we are involved in it. Stepping back from an issue or matter will enable you and the team to discuss the implications of the situation. A collective discussion will give a better understanding than a one-person driven outcome. Asking your employees to 'step back and think about this in a bigger context' can really improve the outcome.

Stepping back can help you move forward and ensure the right people are involved. Sometimes it makes you realise that the problem is not yours at all.

Ask, what do you need from me?

As leaders, we have neither the time nor need to be involved in every conversation or problem. It's simply not possible. Seeing our role as an enabler of conversations shifts our focus from the problem-solver to the facilitator of change. This is a major attribute for successful leaders.

If we see our role as a fixer, we fail to let go and get caught up in the detail because we don't trust others to sort it out. This is a distraction. When we trust our team, we enable others to own projects and discussions, releasing ourselves from detail and opening up opportunities for the team to get more involved. It builds trust and ownership.

Asking 'What do you need from me?' not only demonstrates that you trust that person but also creates engagement as it empowers others to own the project and take pride in the outcome. Meanwhile, we can focus on making sure things happen – without doing them ourselves.

This is exactly where we should be as leaders in the 2020s: coaching and enabling others to succeed and relying on trust to empower employees.

REFLECT

Five Takeaways:

- There are four types of conversations that enable leaders to build trust and engagement
- *Why* conversations reinforce the organisation's vision and purpose using logic
- *What* conversations clarify team direction with explanations and discussions
- *Who* conversations clarify roles and responsibilities
- *How* conversations create ideas and solutions.

Three Questions:

- How are you using the triangle of trust to guide your team conversations?
- What rituals and rhythms are you building that will help you lead the conversation?
- How are you ensuring that your conversations empower others rather than telling them what to do?

One Quote:

> ❝ Building trust is like putting rocket fuel in your tank. It is a catalyst that enhances performance and helps us go further faster. ❞
>
> – Paul Matthews

Conclusion

When I woke half-dead in a ditch in India, I had no real option but to trust others. It was the only possible choice.

As leaders, we make daily choices about how we communicate and engage, and whether or not to trust others. Building trust into how we lead is vital for our success in these times. Our employees expect us to be human, so our choice to evolve and meet their needs is already made for us. Unless we evolve, we will not survive, let alone thrive.

The common goal for all leaders is to unite employees and achieve goals. If we want to connect then trust is the best available strategy. Choosing trust over telling makes our employee interactions more real and more relevant and aligns with the needs of our business. Trust is our opportunity to create breathtaking results across our entire organisation every day.

Switching to trusting is entirely in our sphere of control. It's a choice that I want to make easier for all leaders. That is why I have laid out the signposts, resources and best route to take when you switch.

Like any change, once you start, you'll gain momentum. Eventually, you will create your own way and habits and take pride in your results. The really rewarding part is when you see how trust comes home in the form of improvements, team pride, greater effort, productive relationships and achievements. That is what really makes leading in this way worthwhile and rewarding.

When we commit to trusting conversations, learn about our employees, align our agenda and conversation infrastructure, we have all the tools at our disposal to make a significant change.

I once decided to remove a senior manager working in my team. It was a decision I took very seriously – it's one every leader dreads, avoids or puts off. I chose to involve and engage the manager consistently in the process. That connection ensured my communication was aligned to their situation. Our consistent conversation made the process more manageable for both of us. At our final conversation (the big one!) the manager confided in me that whilst my decision was hard to accept, they believed that trusting them had made it much easier. Despite their termination, they still trusted me. It made the entire situation more palatable. We parted company knowing that we still had a future and respect for each other as human beings. This reinforced trust with others in the team too. It showed me that trust could transcend even the most difficult decisions we are called on to make as leaders.

Humans need trust to survive and thrive at work and at home. We used to rely on authority and control to get things done, but now we know better. The evidence and examples outlined in these pages demonstrate a much better way to communicate and lead others. One that is directly aligned to human nature and that maximises their performance and effort at work.

Trust is not just a person-to-person choice. Collectively our businesses can build whole cultures of trust that magnify results dramatically. That is my ultimate goal for Switch, that every leader builds trust into how they lead so that others are confident to do the same.

Choosing trust is our collective opportunity to make a significant improvement for the future. Consider it as a way to renew your leadership style with a workforce that is screaming out for more involvement and connection. Putting trust in the tank is an investment that will yield rewards for the long journey ahead.

It allows every leader in every business to break the accepted norm of low trust in management. This is the final frontier of effective leader communication. Your trusting conversations, not your telling, is what will enable you to succeed, standing out from other leaders that tell, control and limit.

Evolving and trusting is the essence of leadership for the 2020s.

About the Author

Paul Matthews believes trust is the essence of leadership. Powerful and trusting communication unleashes limitless potential in ourselves and others. That is why he obsesses over helping leaders involve others so that they can raise the roof on their impact and results.

After two decades of working in complex businesses (clinical, logistics, infrastructure, unionised, male-dominated, manual and corporate environments), Paul now runs his own practice supporting leaders to ignite employee ideas, effort and change through communication.

He helps leaders implement strategy by uniting teams and switching them on. His approach is valued in UK and Australian businesses, where he has mentored leaders to mobilise workforces of more than a million employees in culture and behavioural changes.

The leaders Paul works with become more aligned to the needs of their teams and workforce. As a result, they see positive growth in engagement scores, enhanced operations, better employee relations, reduced turnover and higher customer scores. Their teams also become happier, humanised and more involved because their leaders trust them.

For more information about Paul and to find out how he can support your growth, go to paulmatthews.com.au

You can also sign up to his regular updates on all things leadership, culture and communication at www.paulmatthews.com.au/subscribe

Email Paul at paul@commscoach.org to start a conversation.

References

Balboa, N. a. G. R. D., 2019. *The Neuroscience of Conversations.* [Online]
Available at: https://www.psychologytoday.com/au/blog/conversational-intelligence/201905/the-neuroscience-conversations
[Accessed 2020].

Branson, R., 2015. *My top 10 quotes on communication.* [Online]
Available at: https://www.virgin.com/branson-family/richard-branson-blog/my-top-10-quotes-communication
[Accessed August 2020].

Deloitte, 2019. *From employee experience to human experience.* [Online]
Available at: https://trendsapp.deloitte.com/reports/2019/global-human-capital-trends/from-employee-experience-to-human-experience.html

Dolan, G., n.d. *Gabrielle Dolan.* [Online]
Available at: www.gabrielledolan.com
[Accessed 2020].

Dollard, C., 2018. *Emotional Intelligence Is Key to Successful Leadership.* [Online]
Available at: https://www.gottman.com/blog/emotional-intelligence-key-successful-leadership/
[Accessed November 2020].

Edmondson, A. C., 2018. *The Fearless Organization: Creating Psychological Safety in the Workplace for*

Learning, Innovation, and Growth. Hoboken, NJ: John Wiley & Sons.

Enterprise Agility, 2017. *Counting the cost of inefficient communication.* [Online]
Available at: https://www.raconteur.net/sponsored/counting-the-cost-of-inefficient-communication/
[Accessed 2020].

Entrepreneur, 2017. *How Emotional Intelligence Can Improve Your Productivity.* [Online]
Available at: https://www.entrepreneur.com/article/296888
[Accessed November 2020].

Feser, C., Mayol, F. & Srinivasan, R., 2015. *Decoding leadership: What really matters.* [Online]
Available at: https://www.mckinsey.com/featured-insights/leadership/decoding-leadership-what-really-matters
[Accessed August 2020].

Forbes, 2010. *Start Smiling: It Pays To Be Happy At Work.* [Online]
Available at: https://www.forbes.com/2010/08/13/happiest-occupations-workplace-productivity-how-to-get-a-promotion-morale-forbes-woman-careers-happiness.html#41d82b8defb4
[Accessed 2020].

Gallup, 2017. *https://www.gallup.com.* [Online]
Available at: https://www.gallup.com/workplace/238079/state-global-workplace-2017.aspx
[Accessed August 2020].

Gandhi, V., 2018. *Want to Improve Productivity? Hire Better Managers.* [Online]

Available at: https://www.gallup.com/workplace/238103/
improve-productivity-hire-better-managers.aspx
[Accessed November 2020].

Giles, S., 2016. *The Most Important Leadership
Competencies, According to Leaders Around the World.*
[Online]
Available at: https://hbr.org/2016/03/the-most-
important-leadership-competencies-according-to-
leaders-around-the-world?utm_medium=social&utm_
campaign=hbr&utm_source=linkedin
[Accessed 2020].

Goleman, D., 2000. *Leadership That Gets Results.* [Online]
Available at: https://hbr.org/2000/03/leadership-that-
gets-results
[Accessed 2020].

Goleman, D., 2004. *What Makes a Leader?.* [Online]
Available at: https://hbr.org/2004/01/what-makes-a-
leader?
[Accessed 2020].

Goleman, D., 2011. *The Must-Have Leadership Skill.* [Online]
Available at: https://hbrascend.org/topics/must-
leadership-skill/
[Accessed 2020].

Goleman, D., 2013. *Focus: The hidden driver of excellence.*
New York: Bloomsbury Publishing.

Google, n.d.. *Guide: Stay technical and results-focused.*
[Online]
Available at: https://rework.withgoogle.com/guides/
managers-stay-technical-and-results-focused/steps/
introduction/
[Accessed 2020].

Hastie, E., 2020. *Shorter work weeks could be embraced by more companies in Australia.* [Online]
Available at: https://www.news.com.au/finance/work/at-work/shorter-work-weeks-could-be-embraced-by-more-companies-in-australia/news-story/312b35bedddf1df2c77483e8e7269572
[Accessed 2020].

Lewis, P., 2020. *The poll surprise is that Scott Morrison's popularity hasn't taken an even bigger hit.* [Online]
Available at: https://www.theguardian.com/commentisfree/2020/jan/14/the-biggest-poll-surprise-is-that-scott-morrisons-popularity-hasnt-taken-an-even-bigger-hit
[Accessed August 2020].

Lytkina Botelho, E., Rosenkoetter Powell, K., Kincaid, S. & Wang, D., 2017. *What Sets Successful CEOs Apart.* [Online]
Available at: https://hbr.org/2017/05/what-sets-successful-ceos-apart?utm_source=linkedin&utm_medium=social&utm_campaign=hbr
[Accessed 2020].

McCrindle, n.d.. *Changing Generations.* [Online]
Available at: https://2qean3b1jjd1s87812ool5ji-wpengine.netdna-ssl.com/wp-content/uploads/2018/03/GenZGenAlpha.pdf
[Accessed November 2020].

Mindvalley, 2019. *Mindset Definition: How Your Mindset Sets the Stage.* [Online]
Available at: https://blog.mindvalley.com/mindset-definition/
[Accessed 2020].

Minor, D., Brook, P. & Bernoff, J., 2017. *Data From 3.5 Million Employees Shows How Innovation Really Works.* [Online]
Available at: https://hbr.org/2017/10/data-from-3-5-million-employees-shows-how-innovation-really-works
[Accessed 2020].

Mitchell, S., 2017. *Decathlon's staff-driven secret to success.* [Online]
Available at: https://www.afr.com/companies/retail/decathlons-staffdriven-secret-to-success-20170527-gweo9a
[Accessed 2020].

Morse, B., 2018. *Emotional Intelligence Guru Dan Goleman Said the Best Leaders Always Do This.* [Online]
Available at: https://www.inc.com/brit-morse/why-emotionally-intelligent-leaders-follow-their-gut-according-to-daniel-goleman.html
[Accessed November 2020].

Nhaissi, E., 2019. *Feelings And Their Place At Work.* [Online]
Available at: https://www.forbes.com/sites/theyec/2019/12/03/feelings-and-their-place-at-work/#4f8d00742d45
[Accessed 2020].

Palacio, X., 2019. *ESOMAR's latest Global Market Research report values global research and data industry market at US $80 billion.* [Online]
Available at: https://www.researchworld.com/esomars-latest-global-market-research-report-values-global-research-and-data-industry-market-at-us-80-billion/
[Accessed November 2020].

Pendell, R., 2019. *8 Behaviors of the World's Best Managers.* [Online]
Available at: https://www.gallup.com/ workplace/272681/habits-world-best-managers. aspx?utm_source=workplace-newsletter&utm_ medium=email&utm_campaign=WorkplaceNewsletter_ Jan_01072020&utm_ content=doyourmanagershavethem-textlink-1&elqTrackl d=68dd021f3cdd40f5845a30f515bbd19
[Accessed 2020].

Pistrui, J., 2018. *The Future of Human Work Is Imagination, Creativity, and Strategy.* [Online]
Available at: https://hbr.org/2018/01/the-future-of-human-work-is-imagination-creativity-and-strategy
[Accessed 2020].

Ryan, L., 2016. *Command-And-Control Management Is For Dinosaurs.* [Online]
Available at: https://www.forbes.com/sites/ lizryan/2016/02/26/command-and-control-management-is-for-dinosaurs/#410178d324ed
[Accessed 2020].

Sostrin, J., 2017. *To Be a Great Leader, You Have to Learn How to Delegate Well.* [Online]
Available at: https://hbr.org/2017/10/to-be-a-great-leader-you-have-to-learn-how-to-delegate-well
[Accessed November 2020].

The Economist Intelligence Unit, 2018. *Stop dealing with the fallout of poor communication.* [Online]
Available at: https://www.lucidchart.com/pages/research/ economist-report
[Accessed 2020].

Thompson, L., 2017. *Research: For Better Brainstorming, Tell an Embarrassing Story.* [Online]
Available at: https://hbr.org/2017/10/research-for-better-brainstorming-tell-an-embarrassing-story
[Accessed August 2020].

Trimboli, O., 2017. *Deep Listening: Impact beyond words.* Sydney: Self published.

Zak, P. J., 2019. *How Our Brains Decide When to Trust.* [Online]
Available at: https://hbr.org/2019/07/how-our-brains-decide-when-to-trust
[Accessed 2020].